2ND EDITION

DOUGLAS GRAY

Acknowledgements

The publishers acknowledge the kind permission to quote copyright material received from: Addison Wesley, Harvard Business Review and the Institute of Management Consultants.

Publisher's note

Every possible effort has been made to ensure that the information contained in this book is accurate at the time of going to press, and the publishers and authors cannot accept responsibility for any errors or omissions, however caused. No responsibility for loss or damage occasioned to any person acting, or refraining from action, as a result of the material in this publication can be accepted by the editor, the publisher or any of the authors.

First published in Canada and the United States of America by International Self-Counsel Press Ltd, 1481 Charlotte Road, North Vancouver, British Columbia V7J 1H1, Canada in 1985

© International Self-Counsel Press Ltd 1985, 1986, 1990, 1995, 1996, 2002

First published in Great Britain by Kogan Page Limited in 1989 by arrangement with International Self-Counsel Press Ltd, North Vancouver, British Columbia, Canada
Second edition 2004

© Kogan Page 1989, 2004

Kogan Page Limited
120 Pentonville Road
London N1 9JN
United Kingdom
www.kogan-page.co.uk

The right of International Self-Counsel Press Ltd to be identified as the authors of this work has been asserted by them in accordance with the Copyright, Designs and Patents Act 1988.

British Library Cataloguing in Publication Data

A CIP record for this book is available from the British Library

ISBN 0 7494 4309 X

Typeset by Datamatics Technologies, Mumbai, India
Printed and bound in Great Britain by Biddles Ltd, Guildford and King's Lynn

Contents

Tables

Samples

Introduction

This book is designed primarily for the beginning or potential consultant, but consultants who have been in practice for a considerable time should also find it helpful. The purpose of this book is to provide essential information and practical step-by-step guidelines to assist you in starting and developing a successful and profitable consulting business. All the information necessary to set up and maintain your own business is included in this book.

The book is organized to reflect a typical consulting business, from getting the original idea to generating income sufficient for your needs and expectations. You will assess your consulting potential and determine your marketable skills in chapter 2. In chapters 3 through 13 you will learn all the basic steps you have to consider before starting your business. Chapters 14 and 15 deal with the marketing techniques essential to success. Without effective ongoing marketing, you simply will not succeed. Chapters 16, 17, and 18 inform you how to negotiate a consulting assignment from the first interview to the proposal to obtaining the contract. Chapter 19 shows you ways of effectively managing your time. Chapter 20 discusses ways of expanding your practice.

The tables, samples, and appendices have been provided to make the text as meaningful as possible. There are many good reference books that can assist you further; these are listed in appendix 3: Further reading and have been divided into various section headings for easy reference by subject area. Sources of reference information for consultants are listed in appendix 1. Consulting is basically a knowledge industry, and access to ways of improving your knowledge should assist you in marketing your skill more effectively.

Each chapter in this book stands independently but is linked to the others. If you know little about consulting or being in business, you should read the chapters sequentially to appreciate the need for dealing with basic business considerations. Understanding and managing the business side of consulting is as essential as performing the consulting service.

Every year the demand for consultants increases as our society becomes more complex. Business, education, health care, government, military, trades unions, social services community and volunteer organizations employ consultants on a regular basis. Throughout the whole of the EU, consulting has become a thriving, high-value and high-earning industry.

Consultants are people who are determined to succeed, who thrive on challenge, and who believe in themselves.

Consultants are entrepreneurs in the knowledge field. Consultants are individuals who believe that they are competent and capable of rendering a worthwhile service to others.

Consulting offers a continual challenge and can present opportunities for freedom, growth, and satisfaction far beyond those of employment or other forms of business. This book increases your chance of capitalizing on the opportunities and assisting your business success.

Note: This book aims to highlight common consulting practices accurately. However, the information is general in nature, and no legal, tax, or financial advice is given. If legal or other expert assistance is required, you should obtain the services of competent professionals.

Laws are constantly changing. Every effort has been made to make this publication as current as possible. However, the author and the publishers of this book make no representation or warranties regarding the outcome or the use to which the information in this book is put and are not assuming any liability for any claims, losses, or damages arising out of the use of this book. The reader should not rely on the author or the publishers of this book for any professional advice. Please be sure that you have the most recent edition.

1

Understanding the consulting business

WHAT IS A CONSULTANT?

A consultant is someone who has expertise in a specific area or areas and offers unbiased opinions and advice for a fee. The opinion or advice is rendered exclusively in the interests of the client and can cover the provision of information, assessment, analysis, recommendations, and implementation. A consultant generally works closely with the client's staff, but uses employees, sub-consultants, or others as required for the specific project and in accordance with the agreement. A consultant is not an employee but an independent contractor, usually self-employed, sometimes a member of a consultancy firm or partnership, contracted to perform a short-term or long-term task and paid on an hourly, daily, or project basis or other fee arrangement.

There are numerous consulting opportunities in the private and public sector. Table 1 provides a brief summary of some of the major consulting areas. The consulting profession has grown extensively over the past 15 years and is now one of the major service industries in Europe. The outlook for the continued growth of consulting is very positive. Demand exceeds the projected supply.

The consulting industry prospers in most economic conditions. The amount of income that a consultant can earn is, of course, related to many factors, including the field of knowledge and level of expertise in that field. The degree of profit is also directly related to how effectively time is managed and how efficiently the business is administered. New consultants spend a large portion of time managing the task, researching their field of expertise, improving on techniques, and marketing their expertise. Most of these tasks are essential but unbillable hours.

TABLE 1
MAJOR CONSULTING SUBJECT AREAS

Accountancy

Acoustics

Actuarial services

Advertising

Architecture

Attitude surveys

Audiovisual services

Automation
– Office
– Industrial

Building management

Business administration

Business forms and systems

Cable television

Career guidance

Communication
– Electronic
– Interpersonal

Community relations

Conference and convention
planning and management

Construction services
– Management
– Heating/ventilating/
air conditioning
– Inspection and estimates

Curriculum development

Data processing
– Computer hardware
– Computer software/
programming
– Systems analysis

Direct marketing

Economic research, analysis,
forecasting

Editorial services

Educational services
– Curriculum development
– School/college selection

Electronics

Employee benefit planning
– Pension planning
– Profit sharing

Energy management and
conservation

Engineering
– Aeronautical
– Chemical
– Civil
– Electrical
– Electronics
– Environmental
– Industrial
– Marine
– Mechanical
– Mining
– Nuclear
– Petroleum

Estate planning

Executive development and
recruitment

Exhibition planning and design

Financial management
– Banking
– Budgeting
– Investment counselling

Food facilities design

Food retailing

Food services

Foreign licensing

Forestry

Franchising

TABLE 1 (*Continued*)

Freight transportation and
  shipping

Fundraising

Furnishings

Government relations
- Local
- Regional
- National

Graphic design

Health services administration

Heating

Hospital administration

Hotel management

House publications

Human factors engineering

Human relations

Human resources development
- Employee selection and
training
- Employee surveys
- Industrial psychology
- Personnel productivity

Immigration and naturalization

Industrial/manufacturing services
- Industrial classification
- Industrial development
- Industrial testing
- Production management

Industrial relations

Information technology

Insurance

Interior design
- Colour
- Furnishings
- Lighting

International business and trade

Inventory control

Land use planning

Landscaping

Leasing
- Equipment
- Transportation

Library design and services

Licensing

Lighting

Lithography

Mail order

Marketing programmes and
  services

Market research and analysis

Marriage counselling and family
  relations

Materials handling

Materials science

Mergers and acquisitions

Microforms

Museum and exhibition planning
  and design

National security and defence

Naturalization

New product design

New product introduction

Nutrition

Office design

Office management

Operations research

Opinion polls

Organization analysis and
  development

Packaging

Personal image

Personnel

Planning (long range, strategic)

TABLE 1 (*Continued*)

Political campaigning

Pollution control
  – Air
  – Noise
  – Water

Product design

Professional practice management

Property development and
  management

Public relations

Publishing

Purchasing

Real estate

Records management

Recreation planning

Reliability and quality control

Relocation services

Research and development

Safety services
  – Accident investigation
  – Expert witness
  – Fire protection
  – Product liability
  – Programme design and
    installation

Sales
  – Forecasting
  – Management
  – Personnel recruiting
  – Policy and planning
  – Retail/wholesale

Salvage and reclamation

Sanitation

Security (investigation and
  loss prevention)

Shipping

Small business development

Social services

Sports

Standardization

Statistical services

Stockholder relations

Systems analysis

Taxes

Technology transfer

Telecommunications

Television and radio

Traffic and parking

Transportation planning and
  management

Urban renewal

Utilities management

Venture capital

Wage and salary administration

Warehousing

Women's issues and concerns

WHO GOES INTO CONSULTING?

Basically, a consultant is a person with a marketable skill, a perceptive mind, a need for independence and challenge, an ability to communicate with others and persuade them to follow advice, a desire to help others in an effective way, and a wish to be an agent of positive change. In general, the people who go into consulting include:

▌ People frustrated with their current careers, who see the solutions for problems but are unable to effectively influence decision-makers

▌ People who want a stimulating, dynamic, growing career that satisfies the need for personal development

▌ People dissatisfied with the lack of challenge, opportunity, or creativity in their existing jobs

▌ People graduating from higher education with training but little experience who wish to work for a large consulting firm

▌ People who are between jobs and seeking new opportunities and careers

▌ People who see that they may be made redundant and wish to establish themselves in a business to earn a livelihood; these people may start on a part-time basis while still employed

▌ People who have been made redundant and see consultancy as an alternative to unemployment, at least until a better opportunity arises

▌ Retired people who have expertise and wisdom to offer

▌ People who wish to supplement their present income by using their managerial expertise or technical and academic skills

▌ People with work experience and industry knowledge or other skills who want to combine a family life with work at home

▌ People who understand government operations and the contract process, or who have built up contacts in government, politics, or industry over the years

WHY DO ORGANIZATIONS USE CONSULTANTS?

There are many reasons why the private and public sector need consultants for problem solving. Some of these reasons are discussed below.

Temporary assistance

Clients frequently wish to supplement skills in their organization by hiring trained, proven, motivated consultants on a short-term or long-term basis. Consultants may be hired on a project, seasonal, or new funding basis.

By hiring consultants, clients do not have to contend with the training, instruction, and long-term commitment for salaries and fringe benefits entailed in hiring a skilled employee. Recruitment costs alone for a skilled employee can be considerable and cannot be justified for short-lived or cyclical need. Consultants are independent contractors and therefore no tax deductions or fringe benefits are involved.

Objective review

Consultants are retained as impartial advisers without any vested interest in the outcome of the recommendations. Internal staff may not be able to see the problems or may not be sufficiently objective. A consultant can perform a competent and thorough analysis of the issues. It is easier psychologically for personnel to adapt to external advice rather than the internal advice of someone who may be acting out of self-interest.

Third-party request for problem identification and resolution

Banks are naturally concerned about any signs of a problem that might put their investment at risk. A bank may need to know whether the problems are related to administrative, personnel, financial, market, or product difficulties and how the problems can be solved. Only an outside consultant's opinion would be credible.

Surviving a crisis

A business owner suffering from serious business problems may seek an outside consultant to investigate the causes and recommend solutions.

Initiating change

A consultant can act as a catalyst for stimulating ideas in a highly structured organization that otherwise might be resistant to change because of its size, bureaucracy, and institutionalized nature.

Obtaining funding

Many nonprofit organizations or small- and medium-size businesses need assistance in obtaining grants or loans for their continued survival. They may lack the expertise, ability, or time to research the availability of funding and prepare a persuasive application. Consultants with an expertise in this area act as advisers or agents.

Selecting personnel

A client might hire a consultant for recruitment of key executives. The consultant is looked upon as being independent and unbiased with the expertise and time to selectively screen and recommend prospective candidates.

In-house education

Consultants are hired to provide in-house training to keep staff informed of new management and supervisory techniques or technical knowledge and to improve employee morale.

Dealing with internal personnel difficulties

Outside consultants are retained to review and make recommendations on internal structure, for example consolidation of departments or services or elimination of redundant employees or executives. The consultant's report provides the rationale for making the decisions. The consultant then leaves and is not affected by the decision.

Consultants can also be used to resolve conflicts between various levels of management. The consultant plays an arbitrating or mediating role that permits frustrations to be expressed so that energy can be directed toward constructive resolution.

Delaying tactics

Consultants can be hired to perform research studies which take the pressure off a company that is being exposed to public or government scrutiny. This also permits the organization to use the excuse of a consultant's study to justify a delay in decision-making. The consultant is frequently asked to be the contact person, which reduces media attention on the organization concerned.

Executive assistance

An executive who is aware of his or her personal limitations may request that a consultant review a problem situation, provide advice on how to deal with it, and possibly follow up with implementation.

Government regulatory compliance

Government regulations at all levels are constantly changing, and companies are frequently not prepared or trained to comply. Consultants may be retained to provide expertise to assist a company in complying economically, efficiently, and with the least amount of trauma to the organization.

Socio-economic and political changes

Socio-economic and political matters are always in a state of flux. These changes present opportunities for consultants. For example, pollution problems create a need for environmental protection experts, and fuel shortages create a need for energy conservation experts.

Government excess funds

Consultants benefit considerably from the expenditure of large amounts of government money. The government may be funding the private sector with the hope of stimulating the economy; there may be political reasons before an election; there may be a balance in a department's budget that must be spent before the end of the financial year so as not to reduce the sum requested by that department the following financial year. Governments also frequently hire consultants to assess needs, provide solutions, and to conduct in-house training.

REGULATIONS AFFECTING CONSULTANTS

Some professional organizations are empowered in law to exercise rights of practice, membership, and discipline. However, there is no government control or regulation of consultants as such. The term consultant is similar to the term accountant: anyone can use the word to describe his or her activity without credentials, experience, competence, or accountability.

There are many organizations for specific areas of consulting, but membership is voluntary. These organizations or associations have little power or authority to investigate complaints.

Management consultants can apply to become a member of the Institute of Management Consultants. This group provides guidelines for professional practice.

The benefits of membership of a consulting association include:

(a) Certification status if the consultant meets minimum acceptable standards of skill and knowledge

(b) Opportunities for self-development in seminars and workshops

(c) Interaction and networking with other consulting professionals

(d) Representation of the membership's areas of interest to government and other professional bodies

(e) A code of ethics and code of conduct

(f) Keeping up to date on issues in the area of consulting by means of a newsletter or other publication

2

Self-assessment

INTRODUCTION

Many consultants never do a thorough, honest appraisal of their strengths and weaknesses. If you haven't identified your skills, attributes, and talents, how can you determine your specialist areas and the target market? How will you be able to package and sell your services and take advantage of opportunities? Without this awareness it is difficult to project the self-confidence necessary to operate your business and respond to questions a potential client might ask you.

Most consultants never go through the steps outlined in this chapter, and that gives you a distinct competitive advantage. To know yourself – your strengths and weaknesses – is to have power and a prescription for success.

ASSESSING YOURSELF
AND YOUR MARKETABLE SKILLS

The following exercise is important to help you determine the direction you should take in your new consulting business. For the maximum benefit, take all the time you need to complete each stage. Be honest and candid with yourself. The material you are preparing is for your information and benefit only.

After you have completed the exercise, you will have a comprehensive, detailed, and exhaustive guideline for your successful consulting business. Review it, update it, and modify it on a regular basis. If you have taken the time to thoughtfully complete the exercise, you should feel confident that you have developed a realistic framework for the next important stages of your business development.

SELF-ASSESSMENT

1. Summarize your life history. Review and detail all facets of your past, including work positions, projects you have done, education, qualifications you have obtained, activities such as hobbies and sports, family and personal relationships. Include all the work experiences obtained during summers, weekends, or holidays. Start with the most current period and work backward.

2. List all areas of your special interest, achievement, knowledge, and personal satisfaction.

3. List all your skills, that is, things that you can do. Skills are developed or acquired abilities such as training, administering, researching, and problem-solving.

4. List all your talents. Talents are a natural endowment, often a unique 'gift' or special, often creative, attribute. Frequently a talent is a combination of skills. Think of any evaluations that may have been made about you or comments made by your friends in which your talents were observed, for example.

5. List all your attributes. Attributes are inherent characteristics such as an analytical or enquiring mind, intuition or sensitivity. Various studies have found the following attributes essential to successful consultants:

   ▌ Good physical and mental health
   ▌ Professional etiquette and courtesy
   ▌ Stability of behaviour
   ▌ Self-confidence
   ▌ Personal effectiveness and drive; that is, responsibility, vigour, initiative, resourcefulness, and persistence
   ▌ Integrity, that is, the quality that engenders trust
   ▌ Independence: The successful consultant must be self-reliant and not conform to the opinions of others. The consultant must be able to form judgements in the areas of his or her competence and experience
   ▌ Intellectual competence
   ▌ Good judgement; the faculty of sound appraisal with complete objectivity
   ▌ Strong analytical or problem-solving ability; the ability to analyse, assemble, sort, balance, and evaluate the basic factors of problem situations of different degrees of complexity
   ▌ Creative imagination; the ability to see the situation with a fresh perspective
   ▌ Ability to communicate and persuade, with above-average facility, in oral, written and graphic formats
   ▌ Psychological maturity; the successful consultant is always ready to experience people, things, and events as they really are with their unique individual characteristics; to view them in perspective and to

take the action needed in a calm and objective manner without being diverted from a sound, logical and ethical course by outside pressure
▌ Skill in interpersonal relationships, including an ability to gain the trust and respect of client personnel, enlist client participation in the solution of problems, apply the principles and techniques of change, and transfer knowledge to client personnel; a receptiveness to new information or points of view expressed by others; and an orientation toward the people aspect of problems
▌ Technical knowledge, which means an all-encompassing knowledge of the business and also recognizing lack of skill where it exists and seeking to acquire that skill or employing people with that skill

6. List all the skills and attributes you lack that you believe are necessary for a consulting business.
7. List the skills and attributes you lack related to being a consultant that you believe you can improve; write down how that will happen and how long it will take. Prioritize.
8. Of the skills and attributes that you believe you cannot improve, state how that will affect your consulting business choices, if at all.
9. Speak to friends, relatives, or family members who know you well and whose judgement, candour, and goodwill you respect. Ask them to think about your strengths and weaknesses as they see them, and prepare a list. Also ask them to outline the skills, talents, and attributes they believe you possess and those you lack.
10. Update and modify the personal inventories you previously prepared.
11. Review your list of skills, talents, and attributes and provide specific examples where each trait was used that could have a marketing application in providing consulting services.
12. Place in order the 10 activities that gave you the most pleasure and personal satisfaction. Outline how well you did these activities. Don't over-estimate or under-estimate your abilities.
13. List the top 10 skills or talents, starting with the most important, that you feel are basic to your consulting business.
14. Imagine the type of consulting projects that you would like to do and write them down in detail and why you would like to do them. Then review your notes and identify the skills, talents, and attributes required to successfully complete these projects.
15. Imagine your personal life in the future. What direction are you currently headed in with your family and career, socially, financially, spiritually, and personally? What effect would a consulting business have on your existing lifestyle? Would the long hours and pressure of the first 6 to 12 months create strains on the family? Are you interested in marketing your abilities locally, regionally, nationally, or internationally? What effect will these decisions have on you and the people in your life?

16. Think of all the consulting opportunities that might be available to you. Consultants sell themselves as people who have solutions to problems or needs, so look for problem/need situations. Focus only on existing or potential problem/need situations that relate to your area of interest and consulting expertise.

17. Increase your awareness of additional consulting opportunities by using the following resources.

   (a) The Further Reading section of this book (appendix 3).

   (b) Consulting newsletters will stimulate your ideas on managing your practice, marketing your skills, determining consulting opportunities and keeping current on events related to the consulting industry.

   (c) Magazines and newspapers; you should attempt to read everything you can relating to your speciality and general awareness of current events. Subscribe to trade and professional journals related to your area of interest. Get on all the free mailing lists that are of interest or relevant to your speciality area. Read *The Times*, *Financial Times*, *Guardian*, *Independent*, *Daily Telegraph*, *Sunday Times*, *Observer* and *The Economist*. There are other newspapers, of course, that you might prefer to read, but these provide a general indication of trends and interpretation of important events, all of which could have a bearing on opportunities for your business. There are numerous excellent business magazines which can stimulate further ideas and sources of contacts and information. Browse through your local international news outlet for an indication of the publications available. Another alternative is your public library.

   (d) Consulting and professional associations; contact with the associations will provide you with an opportunity to obtain information related specifically to your specialization from newsletters, publications, meetings, or other consultant contacts.
   If there is a local association of consultants, either of a general or specialized nature relevant to your needs, try to attend a number of meetings and ask a lot of questions.

   (e) Government agencies and publications; depending on the area of your interest, you may want to get on the mailing list of government organizations or departments that have regular publications distributed free or at a nominal charge to the public. The government, of course, is a major purchaser of consulting services, and very large sums of money are expended every year directly and indirectly for that purpose. Sources of procurement and contracts information are outlined in appendix 1.

   (f) Public and university libraries; there is a vast amount of information that is current and accessible for you to research or general ideas in your local public or university libraries.

   (g) Continuing education courses and seminars; universities have continuing education courses pertaining to business and related services. The British Institute of Management, The Institute of Directors and other management or professional organizations conduct small business seminars and workshops on an ongoing basis; numerous publications pertaining to successful small business management are also available.

(h) Competitors; attempt to identify the competitors in your specific field. Determine what their style and method of operation are, how long they have been in business, how they market themselves, what they charge, and who their clientele are, if possible. Try to ascertain why they are successful, if they are, and how you can best distinguish yourself and find your own niche in the market. You want to have your own unique style if comparisons are made between you and your other competitors by a prospective client.

18. Define the consulting service areas that you would like to provide (refer to Table 1 showing the major fields of consulting activity).

19. Identify who you believe could be possible clients and why.

20. Project how you would like to operate your consulting business. List the important stages and time frames of your business over the next year, three years, and five years.

21. List how you intend to market your services; that is, create a demand for your service and make potential clients realize that you exist. This question will be answered in another chapter, but it is helpful to go through the reflective exercise yourself.

KEEPING UP TO DATE

Consultants must always be at the leading edge of their discipline. Continuous professional development (CPD) is vital. They should know all about what is happening now and should have a pretty good idea what is going to happen in the future. They have to keep abreast of the latest techniques and be familiar with the newest jargon. If there is a 'flavour of the month' they should be able to talk knowledgeably about it. But they should not leap too hastily on the latest bandwagon. They must believe that there is something in it and should reject passing fads (and there are plenty of these). Above all, they must feel confident that they can use these techniques effectively to help their clients.

Consultants should also know what is happening in the world about them. They should be familiar with economic, political and demographic trends – national and international – and their impact on industry and commerce. To keep up to date it is essential to read professional journals and the quality papers and magazines already mentioned, such as *The Economist*. You should also read key books in your subject area and attend courses and conferences as often as you can afford them (they are a potential source of contacts).

The internet offers a wide range of bulletin boards, forums and conferences within which are discussed numerous topics of professional and technical interest, in addition to newsgroups on consultancy issues.

3

Setting up your business

You have now assessed your skills, attributes, and abilities and have determined your area of interest and expertise. Various administrative matters have to be understood, considered, and dealt with before embarking on your road to success.

This chapter and the next ten chapters deal with the administrative fundamentals. The challenging and fun part – that is, successfully marketing your consulting business – is explained later.

Before setting up your office and opening your doors to the public, many matters have to be considered. Your fee structures, marketing plan, and business plan, which includes your cash flow projections, will all determine how much revenue you must generate to meet your overheads. It is wise to be conservative when estimating anticipated revenue and the lead time it will take to reach a break-even point. Your legal, tax, accounting, and financial advisers will influence your initial decisions. These important aspects are covered in other chapters.

This chapter discusses how to establish the basics of an office while controlling your expenses. With thorough review and comparison of the costs of the key overhead areas, you should require minimal capital investment and keep your level of overheads and risk at a safe level.

START-UP COSTS AND MONTHLY EXPENSES

There are many factors that determine what your costs and expenses are going to be, such as whether you are going to use your own home or rent an office, whether you are going to buy, finance, or lease new or used furniture and equipment, and whether you intend to hire staff or do the typing yourself. Your individual finances and needs and your shrewdness and negotiating ability will clearly affect your overheads.

Start-up costs

Start-up costs vary widely depending on your choices and circumstances. Remember that if you are starting from scratch your fee income may be low in the initial months. You may not even generate enough fees to cover your start-up costs and expenses in the first year of operation, when you will be busy marketing and slowly but steadily building up your reputation. You therefore need these preliminary estimates not only for planning purposes but also to indicate how much finance you might need to raise. If you work on your own from home all you may need is an inexpensive computer and printer, a telephone answering machine, stationery, basic office supplies and some advice from an accountant. You could get away with less than about £3,000 if you were careful. But a sole practitioner could easily spend £20,000 or more if he or she purchased a full range of equipment, obtained a considerable quantity of professional advice and launched an expensive marketing and public relations campaign.

Sample 1 is a start-up expense checklist for estimating initial costs of your business. It is important to keep a record of your estimated and actual costs for overhead expenses as well as for your cash flow projections during the start-up and first year of operation. The date to pay column should assist you in scheduling your cash flow or other funds to meet the initial expenses. You should be able to fill in the estimated costs schedule after you have done your research thoroughly. Further details on aspects of start-up costs are covered later.

Monthly overhead expenses

Naturally, monthly expenses will vary widely depending on the type of consulting service you are planning to operate. Sample 2 should assist you in planning and budgeting for your possible overhead expenses.

Personal expenses

Personal monthly overhead expenses obviously influence your cash flow needs and the amount of resources available to invest in your business. When you prepare your business plan (see chapter 6), you will take into account your personal needs. It will be helpful, though, to consider your personal cash flow needs while planning your business expense outlay. See Sample 3 as a guide for detailing your personal expenses.

SAMPLE 1
START-UP EXPENSE CHECKLIST

Expense	Date to pay	Estimated cost	Actual cost
Business announcement or other initial business development including brochures	＿＿	£＿＿	£＿＿
Supplies and stationery	＿＿	＿＿	＿＿
Equipment/furniture	＿＿	＿＿	＿＿
Rental deposit on office (if outside home: first, second, and last months)	＿＿	＿＿	＿＿
Telecomms installation and deposits	＿＿	＿＿	＿＿
Utility deposits (if outside home)	＿＿	＿＿	＿＿
Insurance (health, life, liability, contents, etc.; unless paid monthly or quarterly)	＿＿	＿＿	＿＿
Legal and accounting	＿＿	＿＿	＿＿
Professional or business membership or expenses	＿＿	＿＿	＿＿
Answering service deposit (first and last months)	＿＿	＿＿	＿＿
Fax machine	＿＿	＿＿	＿＿
Computer	＿＿	＿＿	＿＿
Printer	＿＿	＿＿	＿＿
Mobile phone	＿＿	＿＿	＿＿
Other	＿＿	＿＿	＿＿
Contingency	＿＿	＿＿	＿＿

SAMPLE 2
MONTHLY EXPENSE CHECKLIST

Expense	Date to pay	Estimated cost	Actual cost
Office rent and rates (if outside home)		£_____	£_____
Printing and supplies (not paid for by clients)	_____	_____	_____
Equipment (monthly payment and/ or what you need to set aside for future cash purchases)	_____	_____	_____
Preparation of tax return and other accounting expenses	_____	_____	_____
Legal services	_____	_____	_____
Secretarial services	_____	_____	_____
Fax line	_____	_____	_____
Telephone	_____	_____	_____
Internet connection	_____	_____	_____
Utilities (if outside home)	_____	_____	_____
Insurance costs (over 12 months)	_____	_____	_____
Pension contribution if applicable (estimated costs)	_____	_____	_____
Savings (for yourself and your business)	_____	_____	_____
Loan payments	_____	_____	_____
Taxes (including National Insurance or pension plan)	_____	_____	_____
Advertising	_____	_____	_____
Answering service	_____	_____	_____
Professional affiliation fees and subscriptions	_____	_____	_____
Books and reference material	_____	_____	_____
Marketing	_____	_____	_____
Entertainment and promotion	_____	_____	_____
Car expenses	_____	_____	_____
Other travel expenses	_____	£_____	£_____

SAMPLE 2 (*Continued*)

Expense	Date to pay	Estimated cost	Actual cost
Conferences, professional meetings, trade shows	_____	£_____	£_____
Professional development	_____	_____	_____
Salary (what you need to meet personal expenses)	_____	_____	_____
Miscellaneous	_____	_____	_____

SAMPLE 3

PERSONAL MONTHLY EXPENSE CHECKLIST

Budget for the month of

ITEM	BUDGET	ACTUAL	DEVIATION
Food	£ ____	£ ____	£ ____
Housing:			
Mortgage or rent	____	____	____
Council tax	____	____	____
(if owner-occupier)	____	____	____
Insurance	____	____	____
Clothing	____	____	____
Car expenses			
Payment	____	____	____
Petrol	____	____	____
Repairs	____	____	____
Insurance	____	____	____
Utilities:			
Electricity	____	____	____
Heating (if not electric)	____	____	____
Telephone	____	____	____
Other (water, gas)	____	____	____
Personal spending (gifts)	____	____	____
Credit cards (not covered elsewhere)	____	____	____
Personal and other loans	____	____	____
Life insurance	____	____	____
Taxes	____	____	____
Recreation	____	____	____
Travel	____	____	____
Investment, including savings	____	____	____
Donations	____	____	____
Medical and dental	____	____	____
Education (family)	____	____	____
Miscellaneous	____	____	____
TOTAL	**£ ____**	**£ ____**	**£ ____**

SELECTING A NAME

Selecting your business name is an important decision both from an image and a legal perspective. It is essential to be aware of the implications of selecting your name from the outset.

General considerations

Many consultants do business under their own names: for example, 'David Jones, Educational Consultant.' The business card and letterhead stationery would also show the address and telephone number and a brief description of the service. The description could read, for example, 'Research studies and project management.'

Many consultants prefer to use their own name because they are offering a personal service and promoting and selling themselves. The drawback of using your name is that it implies a one-person operation; this could cause a client to doubt your capacity to complete a project if you are ill or injured. For this reason, and by personal choice, some consultants prefer to use the phrase 'and Associates' after their names. This implies a business with more than one person and a resource base of skilled consultants.

Many consultants contract with sub-consultants as required, depending on the job/project. This cuts down on overheads, provides depth and flexibility, and expands consulting contract opportunities. Other name variations include 'Jones Educational Associates' or 'Educational Consulting Associates.'

It is important to describe the nature of the services you are offering and not limit the future development of your consulting service. For example, if you are a hospital consultant, you may not want to state on your letterhead or business card 'specializing in personnel development' if you could receive other spin-off consulting work outside the limits suggested by personnel development. Don't use the word 'freelance,' as it may not project the professional image you want to create.

Some consultants prefer not to use their own name in the firm's name for a number of reasons. One reason is that the consultant does not want an employer to be aware that a consulting business is being operated part time. Another reason is that if goodwill is developed under a company's name rather than an individual's, a higher price might be obtained if the consulting practice is sold.

If you decide to set up your business as a limited company, you must have the name approved by the responsible government department and the name must end in Ltd or Limited. Advantages and disadvantages of forming a limited company are discussed in chapter 4.

Trading name

If you are operating your business under a name other than your own, you are required in most jurisdictions to register your trading name.

Your accountant or lawyer can advise you about the formal procedures for setting up a limited company and the costs of the process.

SELECTING AN OFFICE

Most consultants begin operations out of their homes. As the business grows, the decision might be made to move into outside office space.

Normally consultants go to the client's office, but occasionally clients wish to meet the consultant at the consultant's place of business.

Home office

There are several advantages to operating out of your home. You save money on services, travel and rent. The stress of commuting to work is reduced. You are able to deduct from income tax the portion of your home you are using for business purposes. (The tax deductions you can use when you have a home office are covered in chapter 9.)

Being close to the family is an important consideration for some consultants.

There are also disadvantages to having a home office. You may be distracted by your family members during the work day, or your presence may be distracting to family members. The mix of home and office dynamics could negatively affect your private life. You could turn into a workaholic due to the proximity of your office. Your home might be distant from your clients' offices, which would make it difficult for your clients to visit you. If clients come to your home office on occasion, you would want your home to present a positive impression and not to detract from your professional image. Your home address on your stationery and business card could present a questionable image to prospective clients who may wonder about your business competence. Clients may view you as a freelancer and be more likely to question your fees.

Because of the limitations of working from your home, you may wish to use an accommodation address that will forward mail and provide a telephone answering service. It helps your image if the address is prestigious but, of course, it will cost you more. The *Yellow Pages* list suppliers of accommodation addresses.

Having a personalized telephone answering service as provided by BT and other telephone companies connected to your telephone at home lets you know your telephone calls are being handled in a professional manner whether you are at home or out making calls. By keeping the answering service informed of your schedule for the day, your callers will receive the appropriate response and know when the call might be returned.

Generally, it's not a good idea to use an answering machine; it doesn't present a professional image, callers get the impression that you are a one-person operation (which, of course, you are), and you may be perceived as a freelancer, which has a negative connotation to some.

Office outside home

You may wish to get an office outside your home when circumstances and finances justify it. Having your own office address increases credibility and stature when dealing with clients or prospective clients. Studies have shown that consultants are able to collect higher fees for performing the same work when operating out of an office.

When considering an office location, factors such as expense, image of business address, your proximity to clients, and referral possibilities should be examined. Try to look at your long-range goals over two years and imagine what your office needs might be. It is costly to pay for new office stationery and other start-up costs, and several moves may create an image of instability.

Office sharing arrangement

You may wish to look for an office with complementary professional or business tenants and prospective business clients. You have your own office and generally supply your own personal office furniture, but the rent expenses of the office and the receptionist's salary are shared on a proportional basis by the tenants. The secretarial expenses are negotiated depending on use.

If you do seek a pooling arrangement, try to have a minimum notice period to leave the premises. You may wish to leave due to expansion, inability to pay the rent, or personality conflicts. It is fairly common to have a three-month notice provision. Make sure that the terms of your rental relationship are in writing and signed by the necessary parties before you begin your relationship.

As a general caution, avoid sharing space with a client. You could fall out or the client could attempt to use your time for free or look on you as staff.

Sharing same private office

Two or more people may use the same office space. The parties agree on the costs of furnishing the office, unless it is already furnished, and an agreement is worked out in terms of the hours and days of use. Costs of this arrangement are negotiated on a per use basis.

Office rental package

There are firms in the business of renting packaged office space. There can be anywhere from 5 to 50 tenants or more. Each tenant has a private office, and there is a common reception area.

The office package arrangement is a good source of potential contacts for networking or prospective clients, depending on the mix of the tenants.

Telephone answering and office furniture are frequently included in the package price as well as a nominal number of hours of secretarial time per month. The rental arrangement may be a minimum two- or three-month notice to vacate, or a six-month or one-year lease arrangement. Prices and terms of various office package arrangements may be negotiable if there is competition in that marketplace in your community.

There are several other advantages of an office package arrangement. Other services that might be available to save you considerable money on staff and equipment include:

(a) Postal address – not a post office box number

(b) Postage metered mail for prompt delivery and a professional appearance

(c) Typing and desktop publishing – a variety of typestyles available on computer for letters, reports, invoices, statements, etc.

(d) Secretarial services, including letter composition and editing using correct business language and form

(e) Photocopying – a bond copier with various features including collating could be available to produce quality copies on your letterhead, transparencies, or address labels

(f) Word processing services with the advantage of speed, efficiency, and storage and retrieval capacity

(g) Data management and bookkeeping

Occasional office

You can rent a board room or an office for as short a time as an hour, a half day, or a day. The cost is negotiable. The occasional office space can be found through office rental package services described earlier. Some firms require that you have a telephone answering or professional identity package arrangement with them before you are able to rent occasional office space.

Leased space

Leasing space does have its advantages, and it is most important that you consult your accountant and a competent solicitor familiar with commercial leases before signing anything. You should shop around for space to make sure you have the best arrangement for your needs and to assist you in negotiating.

Some of the clauses to be wary of when you are considering a lease include ones that restrict your ability to sublet or assign your lease, that restrict the use you intend for the premises, or that limit alterations or improvements to the premises; clauses setting out liabilities and duties of the landlord and tenant; acceleration clauses in case of a default; and clauses requiring your personal guarantee if you are doing business as a company.

If you are still interested in signing a lease, attempt to negotiate as many attractive features as possible. All leases are negotiable and there are no standard clauses. Your solicitor can properly advise you and possibly negotiate the lease on your behalf. Never enter into a lease agreement without consulting your solicitor. The following tips will help when you are negotiating your lease:

(a) Rather than negotiating a three-year lease, for example, try to negotiate a one-year lease with two additional one-year options. This way you minimize the risk in the event you cannot afford the lease, or in case you need to expand or the premises are otherwise unsuitable for your needs.

(b) Consider offering the last two or three months' rent as a deposit. If you default the lease and leave before the end of the term, the deposit monies go to the landlord and you are free of any further liability.

(c) Put in the lease that alterations or improvements you intend to make will be at the landlord's expense.

(d) Attempt to get the first few months free of rent as an incentive for you to lease the premises.

(e) Try to get out of paying the last month's security deposit rent if possible. If it is not possible, try to negotiate with the landlord to pay you interest at a fixed rate on the security deposit money.

Another factor in leasing space is the additional expense for furniture and equipment for your office and reception area, plus the additional costs of a secretary or receptionist. All these additional costs have to be carefully factored out to ensure there is sufficient cash flow to justify the commitment.

Equipping an office

Equipping an office is not too expensive if you buy secondhand furniture. You can obtain good used business furniture from bankruptcy sales, auction sales, or through the classified section in the newspaper. The type and quality of furniture that you select will naturally relate to your type of consulting clientele and the image that you want to project.

There are certain basic things you need for your office, including desk, chairs, tables, lamps, bookcases, filing cabinet, calculator, telephone answering device (optional), tape recorder (to record meetings and consulting or marketing ideas), card file and/or address file, postage meter, and briefcase. You will probably also need a computer, printer, photocopier, fax machine, and other communications equipment. Consultants are increasingly using e-mail as an effective means of communication; it is neither time nor place dependent and much less expensive than either telephone or fax.

Here is an overview of some of the main types of communication equipment you should consider.

Computer

It is likely you are already computer literate and possibly have your own computer at home. Your computer is an essential tool that will maximize your consulting capabilities.

Computer hardware refers to your computer, monitor, and keyboard, as well as your printer and modem. A basic desktop computer and/or a portable computer, such as a laptop, may be all you need. Producing documents, giving presentations to clients, working with graphics, maintaining lists of clients or other records, bookkeeping and accounting, or doing other financial calculations such as budgets or forecasts are all tasks that can be accomplished on your computer.

In addition, you may want to use your computer to keep track of appointments and scheduling information, to do project management or estimates, or for access to the internet.

When deciding on what computer to buy, investigate the manufacturer's customer support services and consider the following:

▌ Is there a three-year limited warranty on parts and labour, with a one- or two-day turnaround policy?

▌ Does the manufacturer offer one year of free on-site service, extendible for an additional fee?

▌ Is there lifetime technical support, 24-hours a day, seven days a week, including holidays, via an 0800 number?

▌ Does the manufacturer offer free remote inspection of your system via modem?

To comparison shop, attend computer trade shows, check out various computer stores that offer a wide range of brand names, and read consumer computer magazine reviews of computers. There are many basic computer books available at computer or software stores. Most universities and further education programmes have a range of computer courses available during the evenings and weekends. As a basic rule of thumb, first decide what type of software you need and then purchase a computer that is compatible with the software.

Modem

A modem is a device connected to your personal computer that allows you to send data to and receive data from computers anywhere in the world over telephone lines. A fax modem is a device that lets you send and receive faxes from your computer.

Computer software

As you are probably aware, there is a wide range of software available to meet all your consulting business needs, whether it be for word processing, data or list management, mailing lists, desktop publishing, graphic design, invoicing and accounting, project management, scheduling, information access, or financial projections and spreadsheets. There are new products being released on an ongoing basis, so be sure to comparison shop at software stores. There is an extensive array of highly sophisticated software available at modest cost to save you time, money, and effort. All of this will reinforce the professional image you wish to create and maintain.

Printer

Your printer is probably one of the most important components of your computer system because the quality and appearance of any documents you produce for your clients reflect your expertise. In general, high print quality and high speed mean a more expensive printer. Colour printers are also available. Resolution measures the print quality in dots per square inch (dpi). The higher the dpi, the higher the resolution and the better the print quality. Laser printers have the highest resolution, followed by ink jet and dot matrix printers.

Copier

There are many types of copier available including colour and small portable copiers to meet your growing business needs. Look for features such as length of warranty, service contract options (on-site or designated repair outlet), paper size, enlargement or reduction capacity, quality of resolution, automatic or manual feed, speed (measured in copies per minute), duplexing (two-sided copying), size of paper trays, etc.

Fax machine

A fax machine is an essential part of your communication equipment. You can transmit documents, diagrams, photographs, etc. through the fax machine to an existing or prospective client for instant communication. You can also buy a portable fax if that would be valuable for your type of business.

There are many fax features available, and competition has brought prices down. Fax machines can print on plain paper, with or without a telephone attached. Some features to consider include transmission speed, quality of resolution, contrast levels, and stored memory capacity. This last feature is helpful in case your machine runs out of paper in the middle of a transmission. Other desirable features include:

▌ automatic redial,

▌ stored telephone directory of most commonly used numbers,

▌ polling capability (sends to multiple preprogrammed numbers),

▌ delayed transmissions for cheaper long distance rates,

▌ fax/phone switch, and

▌ management reports (activity reports, message confirmations, error logs, etc).

Office supplies

The basic supplies you need include business cards, letterheads, stationery and printed envelopes, brochures, records for bookkeeping, invoices, filing folders, and various types of calendar.

Business stationery, cards, envelopes

Your business stationery is very important as it represents you, your image, and your business. It should present a professional and conservative image. It should state your name, your business name, the type of consulting (if applicable), address, post code, telephone number with area code, fax number with area code, e-mail address, and website address (if applicable).

All your stationery should correspond with the format and image of your business card. Choose a good quality paper. Purchase blank pages of your letterhead stock so that your second page will match the colour of the first. Neutral shades such as beige, ivory, or white create a professional impression. You have a choice between litho (flat) or thermo (raised) ink. The raised, glossy appearance of thermo creates a richer effect. The cost of raised letter is not much more than flat, but extra time is required for printing. Because the printing business is very competitive, be sure to compare rates.

Some consultants prefer to have a logo on their business card. Have a graphic artist or desktop publisher design and prepare the logo and other customized material.

Brochures

Depending on the type of consulting practice you have and the nature of the clientele you wish to attract, brochures may be part of your marketing plan. You may choose to have a promotional writer assist you in preparing the text for a brochure that will effectively outline the services you provide for your specific clientele or market. Consider having your brochure designed on a desktop publishing program. Often writers provide desktop layout and design services as well as writing and editing. Such services can be found under the 'Sales Promotion Consultants' section of the *Yellow Pages*. For printing, check for competitive rates and allow yourself considerable lead time to obtain the best rate. One colour ink on coloured paper is less expensive than two inks and can be just as effective. Naturally, brochures are less expensive by quantity.

Record-keeping documents, invoices and file folders

These items are necessary for the orderly maintenance of projects, systems, and good business management. The types of record-keeping documents are outlined in chapter 8.

Calendars

For recording appointments, telephone calls, and deadlines you should have a desk diary, a wall calendar, and a daily diary that you carry with you. The time that you spend on client files must be recorded in detail for proper invoicing and for your protection in the event of a dispute.

Personnel
Secretarial staff

Most new consultants do not have the workload or cash flow to justify hiring a secretary. Some consultants prefer to type documents and correspondence themselves, but even if you are a good typist, you will make more money consulting or finding new clients than you will typing. Some consultants have a family member do the typing, but this can cause strains on the family relationship.

It is far more cost efficient and practical to 'rent' a secretary. In many cases, the typing costs related to a client file can be invoiced directly to the client, in addition to your fees. You then have verification from the typing service if there is any question on your account.

Find a professional typing service that offers temporary or one-time service. Ask how much lead time is required, what the turnaround time is, and what other services they offer. Interview several professional typing services and ask to see sample copies of their reports, newsletters, and correspondence so that you can judge the professional quality of the work.

It is essential that word processing services be available. As a consultant, you will be producing large quantities of material that requires neat, clean, and correctly styled typing. A computer can produce this quality and store your contracts, proposals, form letters, reports, and mailing lists for retrieval.

A professional secretarial service can also look after all your correspondence and document needs including preparing invoices and reminder letters for your receivables. You can ask the secretarial service if one staff member will work on your file so that person will become familiar with your style. A tape for transcription is a considerable benefit in terms of consistency and time saved when one person gets accustomed to your methods.

Retaining other consultants

Employing another consultant as an independent contractor – in other words, a sub-consultant – is a common technique to reduce overheads and increase your resource base and efficiency. There are times when you might need specialized skills or additional help to be able to satisfy a potential client contract. Try to develop a subcontracting network of consultants you can call on when needed. Many consultants take on projects they could not complete themselves and subcontract portions to another consultant.

It is important to maintain your position with your client as the main source of information and communication. Your client need not know that you have subcontracted out a part of the job.

SELECTING A TELEPHONE SYSTEM

Your telephone, in many ways, is your lifeline to a successful consulting practice. Many consultants start out using their home telephone number and a telephone answering device, but there are problems with this.

Inexpensive alternatives exist. The important consideration is the impression your telephone system gives your clients or prospective clients and how effectively you receive incoming messages.

A separate telephone at home

Many consultants operating from home prefer to have a separate line for their consulting practice. This saves the frustration of having children answer your business telephone or family members tying up the line with their personal calls.

Answering service

You may wish to have an office number that does not go to your home, but terminates at an answering service. Your answering service could then phone you at home (if those were your instructions) and advise you of a phone message.

SPECIAL TELEPHONE FEATURES

There are many invaluable telephone feature options available to create an impressive and positive professional business image. They will also save you time and money and improve your efficiency. Ask your telephone company for a current list.

Call waiting

The call waiting feature emits a beep when you are on the phone to tell you another caller is trying to reach you. If you have a custom phone, it allows you to put one call on hold, answer the second call, and switch back to the first caller.

Call forwarding

Call forwarding allows you to send your calls to another phone number or pager, either automatically, if not answered within three rings, or if your line is busy. You never miss incoming or expected phone calls.

Three-way calling

This is similar to a conference call feature. It allows you to talk to people at two or more locations at the same time.

Speed calling

This feature allows you to place a call with a one-digit code.

Phone/fax

A combination phone/fax provides a separate number for your fax machine, even though it uses the same telephone line. You still have your regular phone number. The phone and fax cannot be used at the same time. Your fax machine, if attached to your regular phone line, can identify that a fax message is being transmitted. If you are using a fax frequently, you may want to have a separate line, otherwise you will frustrate your clients. In addition, if you have a home office, a separate fax line solves the problem of your telephone ringing in the middle of the night because of a fax transmission.

Call display

Call display (or call ID) shows you an incoming caller's number on an electronic display screen before you answer the phone.

Name display

This is an added option to call display that identifies the name of a caller.

Call return

Call return lets you know when a busy line is free and lets you return the last call placed or received at the touch of a button.

Call again

The call again feature keeps trying a busy number for you for up to 30 minutes. It rings when the busy number is free.

Call answer

This feature automatically answers calls if you are on the phone or unavailable.

SAVING MONEY ON LONG DISTANCE PHONE CALLS

Some tips

If you are placing long distance phone calls on behalf of a client, ask the operator to call you back with time and charges. This will allow you to record the call in your record system so that the expenses can be passed on to your client directly on the next bill. If you do not adopt this system, you won't be able to render an account to a client for various long distance phone calls until you receive your telephone bill.

To limit the costs of long distance phone calls on behalf of the client, you may wish to ask the client (and confirm it in writing) for the authority to bill to the client's phone number any calls pertaining to your contract or consulting project.

A technique for saving money on long distance phone calls that are being made for information or marketing purposes is to place a long distance phone call person-to-person at 12:30 pm. In many cases, senior people are not in their offices at this time; a message is left by your operator with the recipient company, giving your name and phone number and operator call back number. Also leave a message through the operator about the time and day that you will be in to receive the phone call. State the recipient's time to eliminate confusion.

It is very rare for the recipient caller in government or industry to return your call on a reverse charge basis. You can make sure that you are in your office or home when the incoming call is expected, and you won't have to pay the long distance phone charges.

OTHER COMMUNICATION OPTIONS

Telephone answering devices

The purpose of a telephone answering device (answerphone) is to help you avoid losing critical calls if you are away from your office. It also acts as an efficient office screening agent. The machine answers the phone, gives a message, and accepts a message from the caller on your behalf.

There are six basic kinds of answering machine. Due to the intense competition in this market area, comparative pricing is recommended if you are in the market for an answerphone.

(a) Announce only answers the telephone with one or more pre-recorded announcements up to several minutes long.

(b) Announce/record gives a pre-recorded message and allows the caller to leave a message.

(c) Call screening helps you avoid unwanted calls. By turning the volume higher, you can listen to a caller's message without his or her knowledge. If you wish, you can pick up the telephone, interrupt the regular answering cycle, and talk to the caller.

(d) Record can record a conversation. This is useful if you need proof that you have communicated important information to another party. In many countries you are obliged by law to notify the other party that the call is being recorded. For this reason, some of these machines may emit a tone at intervals to remind both parties that the conversation continues to be recorded.

(e) Dictation allows you to dictate messages for subsequent transcription. You bypass the normal use of the telephone answering machine and use features exactly like those of an office dictation machine.

(f) Remote control allows you to transmit a signal from any other phone by means of a remote device. The machine will automatically respond and play back over the phone any messages that have been recorded. This is convenient if you are out of the office but expecting calls.

As mentioned earlier, telephone answering devices have their limitations. They can create an impression that you are very much a beginner in business and still struggling. Some callers find it very annoying to talk to an answering machine; others refuse to leave a message or leave a message that is unclear. Therefore, you may prefer to consider other options, such as voice mail or an answering service.

Voice mail

This is an effective means of communicating for many businesses. It is similar to a telephone answering machine in various limited aspects, but is far more versatile.

Most telephone companies offer this feature, although generally with just a few menu options for the person phoning. Each menu option involves a separate voice mailbox that is interconnected. There are voice mail companies that can customize features and create new options for you (eg, pressing a specific number on the phone to be connected to your associate, to receive a fax, to have you paged, etc.).

You can also buy your own computer software voice mail system. Many plans offered through a packaged office or business centre service also provide this option. The following are some of the key benefits of voice mail:

▌ Operates all the time, 24 hours a day, seven days a week.

▌ You can call-forward your regular phone number to the voice mail numbers so that it connects automatically. The advantage of this is that you won't have your sleep interrupted by someone phoning you in the middle of the night, as you would if you had a regular answering machine. For example, you may have international clients who live in different time zones.

▌ Reduces frustrating games of 'telephone tag' because it gives the caller the opportunity to leave a message.

- If you are out of town, you can phone your voice mail in the evening to benefit from lower long distance rates when you retrieve messages.

- Voice mail can be connected to your pager or mobile phone, or be programmed to phone you at your regular phone number or at another phone number if a message is left. (See chapter 19 for additional tips and benefits of voicemail service.)

Free-phone number

You may want to consider obtaining an 0800 telephone number if the nature of your business involves existing or potential clients phoning you long distance. For example, if you offer public seminars across the country, people prefer to phone an 0800 number rather than incurring long distance charges. You could have the number directed to a 24-hour, seven-day answering service that will take the registration details and charge card information. In many cases, telephone companies charge a nominal basic monthly fee for the number, and in addition you pay only actual usage charges with no minimum charge. However, you are also entitled to time-of-day discounts as well as volume usage discounts. The net effect could be affordable, efficient, and profitable, depending on your needs.

Generic telephone number

Some business cards have more numbers than a lottery ticket. The caller may not know the right number to reach you. Are you available at your office phone number, pager, voice mail, or mobile number?

Many telephone and other companies offer a single phone number that can direct calls anywhere you want them to go, for example your office, home, car, mobile, voice mailbox, out-of-town hotel number, or anywhere in the world. If you are busy or unable to take a call, your caller can leave a message. There are also other features available such as call screening (you receive only the calls you want), call connection (caller waits on the line while you are paged to any touch-tone phone), and call director (gives your caller a choice of destinations, for example 'Press 1 to speak to the receptionist, 2 to speak to customer service, or hold the line to leave a message'). Some generic numbers also have a fax mail feature that can automatically recognize a fax transmission and store it for future confidential retrieval from any fax machine.

Fax on demand

This feature allows you to programme an option onto your outgoing voice mail message that lets the caller activate an immediate fax transmission.

The caller inputs his or her fax number on a touch-tone phone and your fax message is sent to the caller's fax machine. You can store any number of pages for transmission on your computer. If you have a consulting business that sells products or gives seminars, for example, you can save time by sending out current information for routine enquiries.

Pager

Pagers can be an ideal way to be notified when someone is attempting to reach you by phone. You can buy, rent, or lease pager units. They are small, light, easily attached to your belt or your pocket, and can notify you that you have a message with an audio tone or a beep, or with a visual or vibrating alert. Pager services are available through telephone or private pager companies. There are three main types of pagers:

(a) An alphanumeric pager can receive and display complete text messages of a phone call and up to 40 messages of 80 letter or number characters each.

(b) The numeric pager displays the caller's telephone number and allows you to screen calls for immediate call back when necessary.

(c) The voice pager provides full audio messages with hands-free operation, thereby reducing the need for call back.

Mobile phone

You may want to consider a mobile phone for your business needs. Due to intense competition in this industry, prices have gone down as the number of features available have gone up. There are also many air-time volume discount packages available. Rather than giving a client direct access to your mobile number, you may want to have a pager that records messages left on your mobile or telephone voice mail and then notifies you. This is effective for urgent messages or time-sensitive callers. Alternatively, you could call up your voice mail from time to time to retrieve messages from your mobile. That way you control phone usage and costs more effectively. You also minimize unexpected or unwanted interruptions. For example, you may decide to return a client's call from a regular phone or pay phone. Mobile phone features that are available include:

■ call forwarding,

■ call waiting,

■ three-way calling,

- transfer to a voice message centre and/or voice mail if no answer on your mobile,
- kits for your car to permit hands-free use, and
- detailed billing.

You can also buy mobile phones that have the compatibility to support two-way data and fax communications. Such a mobile phone could be connected to a portable fax machine or computer with a fax and/or computer modem to send and receive data.

E-mail

With your computer, you can transmit messages over the phone lines to someone else's computer through electronic mail (e-mail). You need to know the recipient's e-mail 'address' or password to access his or her computer. The message you send remains stored in computer memory until he or she retrieves it. Conversely, you need to provide your own password so that the person you have e-mailed can reply. Many people have their e-mail address printed on their business cards. Communicating via e-mail can be appropriate in certain consulting situations because it is speedier than letters, faxes, couriers, or telephone. In addition, you can attach documents easily to the e-mail. However, since the work you do for many clients requires confidentiality, for liability reasons you may not want to use e-mail for all your client communications. If you are considering using e-mail, it would be beneficial to have a high speed internet connection, which can be provided by your telephone or cable company. (See chapter 19 for a discussion on additional uses and benefits of e-mail.)

Website

The internet is an online computer network that links many other networks. This 'network of networks' is estimated to join millions of computer users worldwide, and it gives its users access to an incredible amount of data and information. The internet is a cornucopia of information, not all of it useful. There are research, communication, and marketing opportunities on the internet. If you aren't already acquainted with it, you should at least explore the possibilities.

To fully utilize the massive marketing benefits of the internet, you should consider developing your own website. The next section will discuss some of the issues about developing your own website.

DEVELOPING YOUR WEBSITE

For marketing and professional image purposes, you may wish to develop your own website.

Think carefully about two things: the nature of the medium, and your audience. If you are designing a website, or evaluating a competitor's site, you should consider the following points:

❚ Who are the readers?

❚ Why would they visit the site?

❚ Do they have common questions, needs or concerns?

❚ How can you best communicate with them?

❚ What would make them come back?

As an exercise, it might be useful to write down an answer to each of the above questions, and keep your responses in mind when evaluating your own site.

Pitfalls to avoid

What would make you not return to a website? Would you re-visit a site where:

❚ the page crashed your browser?

❚ the screen was difficult or impossible to read?

❚ the design or content was ugly or offensive?

❚ the information was useless or inappropriate?

❚ the content was stale or obsolete?

❚ the site was difficult to understand or navigate?

What annoys you says a lot about you. Did your own list of objections focus on page elements that annoy you: blinking text, too many advertisements, distracting animations, or whatever? Or, did you concentrate on the nuts and bolts of content delivery issues, such as bandwidth limitations and performance issues, or compatibility problems with other software issues?

There are general principles that can help steer visitors to your site in the direction(s) you want them to go:

(a) Most people will follow the first link that appears interesting and, in turn, follow other interesting-sounding links from it as they go. While this seems pretty obvious, it means that you ought to position your 'important' links first. Apparently, web surfers are an easily distracted lot.

(b) Many people have trouble dealing with pages that rely on 'helper applications.' A link to a help page doesn't seem to help too much.

(c) Very few people are willing to 'sign up' to gain access to a page that requires some form of registration, no matter how interesting the content.

(d) The number of complaints about frames (a type of web page constructed from different, simultaneously loaded page elements, arranged in two or more panels) has diminished greatly, as the computer systems are more streamlined and load more quickly. Many people still don't like frames, as they feel they clutter and distract the viewer from the viewing image.

(e) Many people don't like non-black text on a coloured background, no matter how aesthetically pleasing it may seem to you. Although there's the obvious subjective issue of whether they like your choice of colours or not, there are occasional technical issues too. The problem is that you can never be sure how many colours or how many pixels the user has on his or her display.

(f) Web surfers generally use Microsoft Internet Explorer and/or Netscape Navigator browsers. Be sure to test your website to make sure it works with both these browsers, at the very minimum.

(g) The perceived lack of speed of your web page can be a major source of complaint. Be sure to test your site's web pages from a computer running a 28.8 modem, which statistically still represents a significant share of the internet-using audience.

(h) Opinion seems divided on how often you should change your website's design. Some advocate changing design substantially once or twice a year, to keep the look 'fresh' and current. However, even if you never redesign your site, it is imperative that you update your site often – preferably weekly or monthly, depending on your client expectations and the nature of your consulting practice. On the web, nothing is as stale as yesterday's news. Fresh content will also encourage visitors to 'bookmark' your page, for later visits.

The above considerations are all worth thinking about. Of course, you can't please everyone. However, after a few months' worth of feedback from visitors to your site, or from a well-chosen 'focus group' of testers who can critique the site before it is unveiled to the public, you will have received enough feedback to get a sense of what works and what doesn't.

Keeping the website interesting

On business-oriented websites, there are a few categories of content that are consistently popular:

▌ fresh news,

▌ timely coverage and in-depth analysis of almost any topic, and

▌ answers to frequently asked questions (known as FAQs).

For example, your site might provide details of new products or services, a few thought-provoking or informative articles (both your own and from trade journals or popular media), an FAQ section related to your field of consulting, and any upcoming public seminars you might be giving. In addition, you could have a partial list of clients and some client testimonials.

How to design an effective web page

Keep it short. You only have a few seconds to catch a reader's eye. Colour helps. A short list of your top attractions or newest products is better than a long list of everything under the sun.

(a) Short headlines. Keep headlines to six words or fewer. Keep lists to 10 items or under.

(b) Make it interesting. Involve the reader. A description of a product's benefits is always more effective than a list of its features. Remember: explain, don't just describe. Make them think. Invite action and always avoid passive-tense phrases.

(c) Great pictures. In order to get quality pictures to illustrate web pages, the web designer needs to have access to some type of scanner, and a good-quality original.

(d) The big pictures. Don't fall prey to 'clip art syndrome,' where amateur designers litter their pages with several small images. In design work, the secret is to be bold. Make the design stand out and take command of the reader's attention.

(e) Focus attention. When designing a logo or headline, pick the most important word and emphasize it. Make it bigger, bolder, or, if you will be printing in colour, make it stand out.

(f) Simple typefaces. Limit the use of exotic typefaces or, in the case of web pages, graphics that look like typefaces. If angled, warped, stretched, shadowed, or italicized text isn't essential to the message you are trying to convey, resist the urge. Never use an exotic typeface as body text. Don't use more than three or four typefaces in a single page.

(g) Contrast is the key to a successful web design. All emphasis is no emphasis. Never use all capitals in body text. It's okay for short headlines but quickly becomes tiring to read, and never use all caps in cursive script font.

(h) White space helps. Don't crowd every inch of your page with text. Let the headlines breathe. It's especially important to leave plenty of white space around all sides of your page, unless it contains an image that bleeds off the page. As a rule of thumb, leave a white space zone equal to about one-tenth of the size of the design – minimum. It often works well to surround this 'white zone' with a dark border. Research shows that people will look at a page with more white space longer.

(i) Contrast is good. If you are using tables (boxes), follow the rule of thumb about borders in the last tip. Don't overcrowd text in a box that's too small. When legibility, comprehension and retention go up, your page's message is more effective.

In summary, make sure you comparison shop and get quotes from at least five website designers before you make your selection. You need that benchmark comparison and learning curve experience. Do your research on other sites with features you like, so you can tell the designers before they give you a quote. Make sure you have a 'back-end' functionality as part of your website design. That is, you can easily make content changes to the site yourself. Also, your web designer can use existing website template software programs, to customize a site to meet your needs, and save you money in the development process.

4

Legal forms of business structure

INTRODUCTION

There are basically three forms of legal structure: sole trader, partnership, and limited company. You should seek competent legal and accounting advice before deciding on your business structure, as there could be distinct advantages or disadvantages to each depending on your situation.

Many consultants start out as sole traders, as that is the easiest way to start a business. If additional skills or personnel are required on a specific project, sub-consultants may be retained as independent contractors by the sole trader.

In the field of consultancy in particular, a healthy ego is essential to sell yourself and your skills. Because of this, conflict is likely to occur when two or more consultants set up a partnership and share joint decision-making but have individual dreams and goals. It is common for such arrangements to have problems and dissolve.

Forming a company is a third option. The company can be owned by just one person (similar to a sole trader) or two or more people (similar to a partnership).

This chapter discusses the factors that you and your professional advisers should examine when making a decision about your business structure.

SOLE TRADER

If you are working on your own, you can set up in business as a sole trader. It is the simplest form of business structure and operation.

Advantages

Ease of formation: There is less formality and few legal restrictions associated with establishing yourself as a sole trader. You can start almost immediately. There are no complex forms to complete and no documentation required between you and any other party. All you need to do is to inform the Inland Revenue for income tax and National Insurance contribution purposes. If you are providing financial advice or operating a form of employment agency you will also need a government licence.

Cost: Registering the business and obtaining licences involves minimal cost. There are no partnership or corporate agreements required by you because you are the sole owner. Legal fees are reduced accordingly.

Lack of complexity: Operating as a sole trader is straightforward. Unlike other forms of business, there is little government control and, accordingly, fewer reports are required to be filed with government agencies and departments. The owner and the business are taxed as one.

Decision-making process: Decisions are made exclusively by the sole owner, who has complete authority and freedom to move. The owner does not have to obtain approval from partners or shareholders or a board of directors.

Sole ownership of profits: The sole trader does not have to share the profits with anyone. The profits generated by the business belong to one person. The sole owner decides how and when the money will come out of the business.

Ease of terminating/sale of business: Apart from legal responsibilities to employees, creditors, and perhaps clients, you can sell the business or close it down at your will.

Flexibility: You are able to respond quickly to business needs in day-to-day management decisions as governed by various laws and common sense.

Disadvantages

Unlimited liability: The sole owner's personal assets, such as house, property, car, and investments, are liable to be seized if necessary to pay for outstanding debts or liabilities. As mentioned earlier, the sole trader and the business are deemed to be one and the same in law.

Less financing capacity: It is more difficult for a sole trader to borrow money than for a partnership with various partners or a limited company with a number of major shareholders. A lender, when looking for security and evidence of outside resources, can turn to other people connected with the business rather than just the one person operating as a sole trader. A partnership or company can give an investor some form of equity position, which is not available to a sole trader.

Unstable duration of business: The business might be crippled or terminated upon the illness or death of the owner. If there is no one appropriate to take over the business, it may have to be sold or liquidated. Such an unplanned action may result in a loss.

Sole decision-making: In a partnership or a company, there is generally shared decision-making or at least input. With a sole trader, just one person is involved; if that person lacks business ability or experience, poor decision-making can cause the business to suffer.

Taxation: At a certain level of profit there are tax disadvantages for the sole trader.

PARTNERSHIP

A partnership is usually defined as an association of two or more persons to carry on a business in common with a view to making a profit. The partnership is created by a contract, either verbal or written, between the individual parties.

Legislation allowing the formation of limited liability partnerships (LLPs) in the UK came into force in April 2001. Unless the partners are personally negligent, their liability to bear losses is restricted to the assets of the company. The tax treatment of LLPs is broadly in line with that of unlimited partnerships: LLPs will normally be transparent for purposes of tax, with members liable to pay income tax on their shares of profit so long as the LLP is in business. For new practices, the commercial advantages of an LLP make it a potentially attractive business vehicle; but since this is a relatively new form of practice, it is essential to obtain specialist accountancy advice. The cost of registering an LLP with Companies House is currently £95.

Advantages

Ease of formation: Legal formalities and expenses in forming a partnership are few compared to incorporating.

Pride of ownership and direct rewards: Pride of ownership generates personal motivation and identification with the business. The profit motive could be reinforced with more people having a vested interest.

Availability of more capital: A partnership can pool the funds of a number of people compared to a sole trader who has only his or her own resources to draw upon, unless loans are obtained.

Combination of expertise and talent: Two or more partners, by combining their energies and talents, can often be successful where one person alone would fail. This is particularly true if the business demands a variety of talents such as technical knowledge, sales ability, and financial skills. It is important that working partners bring complementary skills to the business, thereby reducing the workload of each partner.

Flexibility: A partnership may be relatively more flexible in the decision-making process than a company, but less so than a sole trader.

Relative freedom of government control and special taxation: Compared to a company, a partnership is relatively free from many restrictions and bureaucratic red tape.

Disadvantages

Unlimited liability: The major disadvantage of a partnership is the unlimited liability except in the case of an LLP. This unlimited liability is much more serious than for a sole trader because all the partners are individually and collectively liable for all the debts and liabilities of the partnership. Each partner's personal assets are liable to be seized if necessary to pay for outstanding business debts.

Unstable duration of business: Any change in the partnership automatically ends the legal entity. Changes could include the death of a partner, or the admission or withdrawal of a partner. In each case, if the business is to continue, a new partnership agreement must be written.

Management of difficulties: As mentioned, when more than one owner assumes responsibility for business management, there is a possibility that differences of style, priorities, philosophy, and other factors will arise. If these differences become serious disputes and are unresolved, the partnership may have to be terminated, with all the financial and personal trauma involved. It is difficult for future partners to foresee whether or not personalities and methods of operating will clash.

Relative difficulty in obtaining large sums of capital: This is particularly true of long-term financing when compared to a company.

Partnership agreement problems: The larger a partnership becomes, the more complex the written agreement has to be to protect the rights and identify the responsibilities of each partner. This can result in additional administration and legal costs.

Difficulty of disposing of partnership interest: To withdraw capital from the business requires approval from all other partners. This takes time and involves legal and administrative expenses.

Partnership agreement

A partnership agreement, sometimes called articles of partnership, is absolutely necessary in a partnership relationship. The agreement normally outlines the contribution of each partner in the business, whether financial, material, or managerial. In general, it defines the roles of the partners in the business relationship.

Some of the typical articles contained in a partnership agreement are shown in Table 2.

If you are considering a partnership relationship, complete the checklist headings and then see your solicitor and accountant. By the time you have completed the checklist with your prospective business mate, the engagement could be off.

Kinds of partners

An *ostensible partner* is active in the business and known as a partner.

An *active partner* may or may not be ostensible as well.

A *dormant partner* is inactive and not known or held out as a partner.

A *secret partner* is active but not known or held out as a partner.

A *silent partner* is inactive and not known or held out as a partner.

A *nominal partner* is not a true partner in any sense, not being a party to the partnership agreement. A nominal partner, however, holds himself or herself out as a partner, or permits others to make such representation by the use of his or her name or otherwise. A nominal partner, therefore, is liable to third parties as if he or she were a partner.

A *sub-partner* is a person who is not a member of the partnership but contracts with one of the partners to represent that partner by participating in the firm's business and profits.

A *limited or special partner* risks only his or her agreed investment in the business assuming that statutory formalities have been complied with. As long as he or she does not participate in the management and control of the enterprise or in the conduct of its business, the limited partner is generally not subject to the same liabilities as the general partner.

LIMITED COMPANY

A limited company is a legal entity, with or without share capital, which can be established by one or more individuals or other legal entities. It exists separate and distinct from these individuals or other legal entities. A limited company has all the rights and responsibilities of a person with the exception of those rights that can only be exercised by a natural person. The cost of registering a limited company with Companies House is currently £20, or £80 for a same-day service.

TABLE 2

CHECKLIST OF ARTICLES IN
A PARTNERSHIP AGREEMENT

1. Name, purpose, and location of partnership
2. Duration of agreement
3. Names and character of partners (general or limited, active or silent)
4. Financial contribution by partners (at inception, at later date)
5. Role of individual partners in business management
6. Authority (authority of partner in conduct of business)
7. Nature and degree of each partner's contribution to firm's consulting services
8. Business expenses (how handled)
9. Separate debts
10. Signing of cheques
11. Division of profits and losses
12. Books, records, and method of accounting
13. Draws or salaries
14. Absence and disability
15. Death of a partner (dissolution and winding up)
16. Rights of continuing partner
17. Employee management
18. Sale of partnership interest
19. Release of debts
20. Settlement of disputes; arbitration
21. Additions, alternations, or modifications to partnership agreement
22. Noncompetition in the event of departure

Advantages

Limited liability of shareholders: Shareholders' personal assets are separate from the business and cannot be seized to pay for outstanding business debts incurred by the limited company. There are exceptions, dealing primarily with the issue of fraud.

Flexibility for tax planning: Various tax advantages are available to limited companies that are not available to partnerships or sole traders. Tax planning must be undertaken with the help of a professional accountant.

Corporate management flexibility: The owner or owners can be active in the management of the business to any desired degree. Agents, officers, and directors with specified authority can be appointed to manage the business. Employees can be given stock options to share in the ownership, which can increase incentive and interest.

Financing more readily available: Investors find it more attractive to invest in a company with its limited liability than to invest in a business whose unlimited liability could involve them to an extent greater than the amount of the investment. Long-term financing from lending institutions is more available since lenders may use both corporate assets and personal guarantees as security.

Continual existence of corporation: A company continues to exist and operate regardless of the changes in the shareholders. Death of a shareholder does not discontinue the life of the company. Continual existence is also an effective device for building and retaining goodwill.

Ownership is readily transferable: It is a relatively simple procedure to transfer ownership by share transfer unless there are corporate restrictions to the contrary.

Draw on expertise and skills of more than one individual: This feature is the same concept as in a partnership, where more partners (shareholders) contribute diverse talents. However, a company is not required to have more than one shareholder.

Disadvantages

Extensive government regulations: There are more regulations affecting a company than a sole trader or partnership. Corporations must report to all levels of government.

Activities limited by articles of association: Articles of association can be very broad or can severely restrict a company's activities.

Manipulation: Minority shareholders are potentially in a position to be exploited by the decisions of the majority of the company.

Expense: It is more expensive to establish and operate a company due to the additional documents and forms that are required compared to establishing as a sole trader or partnership.

Corporate purposes

Articles of association are required to include a statement of the purposes of the company. When you provide a list of the purposes of the company, make sure that you define them expansively. Do not restrict the activity of your company. A general clause should be included allowing the company to expand into any business activity permitted by law. A competent lawyer can assist you in preparing this document to enable you to maximize your corporate options.

Shareholders' agreement

A shareholders' agreement involves the same concepts of protection as a partnership agreement. Many of the provisions outlined in the part- nership agreement are also included in the shareholders' agreement. There are additional provisions frequently covered in the shareholders' agreement, including:

▌ A restriction on transfer of shares

▌ A buy–sell provision that sets out the formula for buying and selling shares in the company

▌ A provision on personal guarantees of corporate obligations

▌ A provision on payback by corporation of shareholders' loans

▌ A provision giving all shareholders the entitlement to sit as a director or nominate a director as their representative. This protects minority shareholders from lack of managerial information and provides them with a directorship vote or veto on corporate decisions. If you intend to be a majority shareholder, you may not wish to volunteer this provision.

Many shareholders believe that articles of association set out the recipe for resolving problems within the company and between the shareholders, directors, and officers in some magical fashion. In most cases, the articles only cover formulas for resolving disputes in a few circumstances. It is the shareholders' agreement that expands the protections to resolve fairly any disputes between shareholders.

If you intend to incorporate and have one or more additional share- holders in your company, it would be wise to obtain your solicitor's advice on a shareholders' agreement to protect your interests.

Legal Forms of Business Structure

Maintaining the corporate protection

One of the advantages of operating through a corporate entity is the protection against personal liability for the debts and liabilities of the company. This is assuming, of course, that you have not signed personal guarantees. However, there are situations that could cause you to be personally liable for corporate debts. Generally, if it can be shown that a fraud was perpetrated through use of the company, or the director totally disregarded the corporate formalities, the advantage of the 'corporate veil' can disappear.

When a court treats the company as a sham and imposes personal liability on the shareholders or directors, it is said to 'pierce the corporate veil.' Here is a list of precautions to follow to prevent personal legal attack.

▌ *Meetings:* A company acts only when its employees (officers, directors, and shareholders) act. If a corporation holds no directors' or shareholders' meetings, the company may not really exist. Therefore, every company should hold at least one shareholders' and one directors' meeting annually and have that fact documented.

▌ *Corporate name:* A business operating in the corporate form must let the general public know that it is a company with limited liability by attaching 'Ltd' or 'Limited' to its name, depending on the form you selected at incorporation. You must specify the corporate designation everywhere the company name appears.

▌ *Acting as agent:* When a shareholder/employee executes a document or engages in a transaction, the person must make it clear that it is being done on behalf of the company. That is, when you sign a cheque or contract, you should write your corporate office title (i.e., president, secretary, etc.) after your name.

▌ *Tax returns:* The company must file an annual tax return and observe the rules for PAYE (pay as you earn) and National Insurance contributions. You must make sure that all periodic reporting requirements are satisfied and that there is never any failure to pay to the Revenue all sums paid by or deductions from the corporate employees.

▌ *Adequate capitalization:* If a company is inadequately capitalized so that there is insufficient capital investment to meet the claims by creditors, the courts may impose personal liability on the shareholders or directors for its business obligations. You should, therefore, be careful that your 'equity' in the company does not become too diluted by loans from yourself and from third parties. As an arbitrary rule of thumb, a debt to equity ratio not exceeding 8:1 is reasonable. However, what is truly 'inadequate' depends on the extent of actual corporate liabilities and the extent of assets to satisfy those liabilities.

∎ *Separate accounts:* Many shareholders of closely held companies treat the company's assets as their own. They combine personal and corporate funds, use corporate funds to pay personal expenses including medical bills and taxes, and generally disregard the corporate 'formalities.' By doing so, however, they run the risk that a court may also disregard the formalities and hold the person liable for the company's debts. The shareholders and directors, therefore, should maintain separate corporate and personal accounts and use the company funds only for business needs.

∎ *Filing Annual Returns:* Companies House requires that you complete an Annual Return listing the shareholders, officers, directors, and current business address of your company, as well as other incidental information. This document must be filed on time to avoid penalties and possible involuntary dissolution. This dissolution could mean that you would be held personally liable for debts of the company.

CHOICE

As a generalization, a small business is probably better off in tax terms being started as a sole trader or partnership. A mature, profitable business may, however, be better off by becoming a limited company.

The choice between setting up as a sole trader or as a partnership is largely dependent on individual preferences and circumstances. Consultants often start as sole traders and, when they are established, form a partnership with one or more congenial people. Quite often, two or three people who have worked together in a normal business or in a consultancy decide that they want to 'put up their plate' and become a consultancy partnership. Alternatively, two people can get together with an idea for a consultancy niche and set up in partnership.

Spouses are often involved, either as employees of the other spouse or in partnership with them. Sometimes a consultant sets up as a sole trader and employs his or her spouse at a fixed salary (and there may be tax advantages in doing so, although PAYE and National Insurance contributions have to be administered). At a later stage it may be considered advantageous from an operational, financial or tax point of view to set up a partnership.

Whatever approach you adopt you should get advice from your accountant on the financial and tax implications and from your solicitor on legal matters.

One of the best sources of information and practical advice on the process of setting up a business in the UK is Business Link, a service managed by the Department of Trade and Industry (DTI). Starting up is just one of a comprehensive series of topics on which guidance can be downloaded from the Business Link website. Other areas of advice include forming and naming a business; choosing and setting up premises; taxes, payroll and returns, including income and corporation tax, PAYE and VAT; employing and developing people; and managing your business, including winning contracts, IT for start ups, marketing and financial control. Business Link also publishes a 'No-Nonsense' guide to government rules and regulations for setting up a business.

5

Selecting business and professional advisers

Since you may be operating on your own, or with a few associates, you will need an extended management team to advise you in specialized areas where you lack knowledge, ability, or interest. Your advisers are, in effect, your employees and associates and should be considered an integral part of management decision-making.

Every business decision involves a legal decision or implication. Every business decision involves accounting, bookkeeping and, at times, tax considerations. The fatality rate of small businesses is enormously high. Statistically the odds are practically ten to one that your small business will not be in business three years after you begin your practice.

This chapter discusses the benefits of the effective use of business and professional advisers, with sections on how to selectively evaluate them and how to use their skills to your advantage.

GENERAL CRITERIA FOR ADVISER SELECTION

How well you select your professional and business advisers will have a direct bearing on your business success. Poor advisers or no advisers will almost certainly lead to your business downfall. Your main advisers are your solicitor and accountant, followed by your bank manager. You should see at least three different people from each of these three professions before you make your selection. It is important to have the comparative assessment.

The following general guidelines should assist you in the careful search and selection of your advisers.

Recommendations

One of the most reliable methods of finding an adviser is by personal recommendation from your existing advisers or friends in business whose judgement and business sense you trust. Bank managers and business advisers who deal on a regular basis with professional advisers are in a good position to pass judgement based on their business dealings. When solicitors, accountants, or bank managers refer to each other, it implies a good working relationship and mutual trust.

Don't rely completely on any referral; make your own cautious assessment.

Credentials

Certification and credentials only ensure that the individual has passed minimum standards of education, training and experience. They do not ensure that the person is a dynamic, innovative, or creative business adviser with a specific amount of experience relevant to your needs.

Clientele

Most professional advisers have a homogeneous client base. Some advisers have many small business clients, others emphasize personal clients, while others go after corporate business. An adviser with a good base of small to medium-sized commercial clients will probably be the most appropriate for your business needs.

Fees

Fees will often vary by the size of the community in which the professional practice is operated, the size of the practice, and the volume of business. You may find that advisers who charge fees in the middle range, edging toward the higher end of the scale, are often quality practitioners in high demand who are still aggressive and innovative in their business practice.

Advisers who are at the low end of the fee scale can be entrepreneurial types, but cut-rate pricing may also indicate a cut-rate, high-volume approach to business that will not suit your objectives. Low prices are sometimes an indicator of low quality, low esteem, or little experience.

Very high-priced advisers tend to be more conservative, less aggressive, and less willing to spend the necessary time with small business clients because their priorities lie with the big firms. Fees vary and many professionals will negotiate them.

It is important to be very open when discussing fees and payment expectations.

Technical competence and industry knowledge

You must satisfy yourself that your advisers are competent in the areas of your greatest need. Ask them how much experience they have had, and how comfortable they are, with your field.

A specific understanding of the problems, needs, and issues of your type of business can enable your advisers to provide the exact assistance you require. This is different from technical competence. It has more to do with experience in a particular type of industry. If the adviser has provided guidance to other small business owners in similar situations, there is an increased possibility that the adviser will be able to provide you with more reliable assistance. For example, if you are a hospital consultant, a solicitor who specializes in or is very familiar with health or hospital law could be an asset to you.

Style and personality

A critical factor in the selection of advisers, beyond simple compatibility, is style. You can have greater confidence in the aggressive adviser who takes the initiative and offers advice before you request it. This style indicates an initiator rather than a reactor, a person who anticipates and performs before matters become serious. It also indicates a creator, an entrepreneur, and a person who can empathize with your problems and concerns. This kind of adviser is more likely to come up with creative solutions to problems and be a complement to your planning function. This type of adviser will not only be a sounding board, but a true part of the management team.

Confidence

You should feel a sense of confidence when relating to your adviser, whether it be in the general sense or in dealing with a specific problem or issue. You should have a certain amount of personal compatibility with your adviser. If you don't, you will probably end up rejecting a fair amount of advice. In other words, if you do not feel that good chemistry exists with an adviser, seek a replacement as soon as possible. If you do not relate well to the adviser, you may hesitate to ask for advice, which could result in some poor management decisions.

Never allow your advisers to treat you in a condescending or paternalistic manner. You should consider them as equals with special knowledge offering a service in the same manner that you are offering a service to your clients.

Communication

You should select an adviser who communicates well, openly and free of jargon. Your adviser should explain the necessary concepts to you so that you understand the issues involved and the decisions that have to be made. Effective communication also means that your advisers forward to you any correspondence sent or received through their offices relating to your business.

Commitment

It is important to sense that your adviser is committed to your best interests and your success. An adviser who is involved with clients that are larger, more important, or higher paying than you are may become indifferent to your needs. You should be alert to this.

Availability

It is important for your advisers to be available when you need them. You are spending time and resources to develop a relationship that will enhance your business decisions. If your adviser is frequently out of town or, in the case of a solicitor, in court on a regular basis, you may not have the immediate access you need. Of course if the adviser is of exceptional quality and ideally suited to your type of practice, some allowances should be made.

Length of time in practice

There is naturally a correlation between the degree of expertise and length of time in practice. You should therefore ask directly how many years of experience your adviser has in the area of your needs.

Ability to aid growth

A good professional adviser will have a history of assisting growth in other clients. The adviser should be able to anticipate growth problems in advance and provide guidance to deal with them.

Small firm versus large firm

Choosing a small or large firm is in many ways a matter of your own personal style and the type of firm you relate to most comfortably. Larger firms tend to be in the central area of town, which may involve parking problems. Their fees are higher. Generally, the larger firms do not have a small business orientation in their marketing and service priorities. The larger firms do have highly specialized advisers and a resource base of associate personnel. This degree of depth may or may not be necessary in your situation. It is not uncommon in larger firms to have small business clients passed over to junior associates or students in training as the more senior advisers handle larger clients.

Smaller firms generally deal with and relate to small business entrepreneurs. Selecting an adviser in a small or medium-sized firm of three to ten people provides you with a resource base if you need it. An adviser who is a sole practitioner may be very busy, too generalized in his or her areas of practice, and lacking a referral resource base within the firm.

Comparison

Make sure you check out at least three advisers before making a final decision. The more selective you are in comparing the personalities, styles, competence, and attitudes of prospective advisers, the more likely it is that you will find someone with whom you can establish a good relationship. Prepare questions for your potential advisers and compare their answers. Assess the quality of answers to your questions, then decide who will be the most benefit to you. Most initial consultations are free; be sure to confirm this when you set up the meeting. The more interviews you conduct, the greater your knowledge base and the greater your confidence that you will choose the right person or firm.

SOLICITOR

There are basically two types of solicitor that you should consider as your advisers. The same person might be able to assume both roles.

You need a solicitor who specializes in small business. A solicitor who cares about small business clients assumes the same role and attitude toward your business health and survival as your doctor to your personal health.

The other type of solicitor you need is one who specializes in contract law. You will need to have several contracts prepared depending on the type and style of service you are providing. There are times you will need to have a specialized contract made up by a solicitor or have the solicitor review and advise you on a contract that has been prepared by the client.

If your business solicitor does not have the expertise in contract law, request that you be referred to someone within the firm or outside who does. For continuity and efficiency, you want to maintain your business solicitor for all matters that don't require additional expertise. You should be able to phone your solicitor as your needs arise and feel confident that the unique aspects of your business are known and understood.

For your protection, you should retain a solicitor before you start up your business, as there are many legal pitfalls that can be encountered. There is a temptation to save money on legal fees in the beginning stages of the business when cash flow is minimal. Some people do their own incorporation to save on initial start-up expenses, but then continue the saving by never obtaining legal or accounting advice, an unfortunate example of false economy and bad judgement.

ACCOUNTANT

An accountant is the other essential business adviser on your management team. It is very important that you retain a properly qualified accountant. A bookkeeper is not an accountant and there is no restriction on anyone using the term 'accountant' and purporting to provide accounting services without proper qualifications or training.

There are many essential services that an accountant can provide. An accountant can advise on all start-up steps of a new business, including the tax and accounting considerations of various types of business organization. Normally an accountant will communicate with or coordinate work with your solicitor. The accountant considers important matters such as when your financial year-end should be.

An accountant can advise on preparing a business plan for a loan application. This includes recommending the type of loan you should consider and how it is to be paid. Documents such as a profit and loss statement, a balance sheet, and a financial statement can be prepared by the accountant. He or she may refer you to a bank, which can have a positive effect on your loan application if the bank manager knows and respects the accountant.

An accountant can advise on all aspects of tax planning and tax-related business decisions which occur from time to time, as well as file your tax returns.

An accountant can advise how to set up your office bookkeeping system. The accountant can have the bookkeeping done by someone in his or her firm at a negotiated fee or you can hire an independent bookkeeper. Your accountant should be able to recommend some bookkeepers.

An accountant can analyse and interpret your financial information, point out areas that need control, and recommend ways of implementing the necessary change.

An accountant may be aware of various government grant programmes that could be of interest to you.

An accountant can coordinate your personal and business affairs and advise you on investments, tax planning and other matters.

An accountant can advise and assist you if you want to change your business or partnership into a limited company at some point. If the transfer is done correctly, you can minimize any negative tax consequences.

BANK MANAGER

Your relationship with your bank and bank manager is your financial lifeline. The process of selecting a bank and banker is a critical one, and substantial comparative shopping is necessary to obtain the optimal combination of personality and knowledge.

Your choice of banker should be considered along with his or her specific experience with your type of business, specific reputation for taking risk, and the demands that are made for security and for reporting results.

Find out the amount of the particular branch's loan approval limit. If your needs are less than the limit, the loan can be approved by that individual without further review by a more senior manager. This means you only have to convince one person to approve your loan request, not additional anonymous people behind the scenes. How well your relationship develops with the manager and how successful you are getting your loans approved will depend largely on the factors outlined in chapter 7 on how to obtain financing.

There are specific danger areas that can affect your bank manager's relationship with you. When the manager changes, there is always a period of risk and uncertainty. The new manager does not want to have any medium- or high-risk loans on the books to taint his or her record. During the first three or four months after a new manager takes over, outstanding loans are reviewed and categorized within the criteria set by him or her. This is the time when loans can be called in or additional security requested or interest rates increased. You should develop a personal relationship with the manager when you take out a loan. If you hear that a new manager has taken over, make a point of quickly introducing yourself and briefly discussing your business in a positive way.

Bank policies change from time to time and your type of business could be looked upon as increasing in risk. If you think the bank is concerned, prepare a realistic assessment of how you intend to deal with the situation in advance. You may have a diversified consultancy, or you may have other options available to that you could explain to your bank.

Ask your accountant and solicitor which bank and banker they recommend. This is probably one of the most effective introductions. If the bank has an ongoing relationship with a professional who is advising you as a client, a less impersonal relationship will exist and there is a better chance that decisions affecting your loans and your business will be made more carefully.

INSURANCE

It is important to select a professional insurance broker with experience and knowledge in the areas of insurance you require. An insurance broker can have various professional qualifications, and you may wish to find out what those credentials are. Insurance is covered in detail in chapter 10.

CONSULTANTS

Private consultants

You may wish to approach a practising consultant for advice to assist you in your business. To protect yourself, you should enquire about their expertise, qualifications, and length of experience. Obtain references and contact them. Apply the general criteria for adviser selection. You will want to satisfy yourself that the consultant is personally successful. If the consultant has not been successful, how can he or she possibly offer advice that will help you?

The local business networks set up under the DTI's Small Business Service can help put new businesses in touch with specialist advisers in most fields of consultancy.

6

Preparing your business plan

WHY PREPARE A PLAN?

Most consultants prefer to be a consultant first and a business owner second. But planning and good management skills are vital to business success. Those who do not plan run a very high risk of failure. If you do not know where you are going in your personal or business life, there is little prospect that you will arrive. A business plan is a written summary of what you hope to accomplish by being in business and how you intend to organize your resources to meet your goals. It is an essential guide for operating your business successfully and measuring progress along the way.

Planning forces you to think ahead and visualize; it encourages realistic thinking instead of overoptimism. It helps you identify your customers, your market area, your pricing strategy, and the competitive conditions under which you must operate. This process often leads to the discovery of new opportunities as well as deficiencies in your plan.

Having clear goals and a well-written plan aid in decision-making. You can always change your goals, but at least with a business plan you have some basis and a standard comparison to use in evaluating alternatives presented to you.

A business plan establishes the amount of financing or outside investment required and when it is needed. It makes it much easier for a lender or investor to assess your financing proposal and to assess you as a business manager. It inspires confidence in lenders and self-confidence in yourself to know every aspect of the business when you are negotiating your financing. If you have a realistic, comprehensive, and well-documented plan, it will assist you greatly in convincing a lender.

Having well-established objectives helps you analyse your progress. If you have not attained your objectives by a certain period, you will be aware of that fact and can make appropriate adjustments at an early stage.

Spending three or four hours each month updating your plan will save considerable time and money in the long run and may even save your business. It is essential to develop a habit of planning and reassessing on an ongoing basis as an integral part of your management style.

FORMAT

The business plan format shown in Sample 4 is a starting point for organizing your own plan. The comments following the sub-headings should help you decide which sections are relevant to your business situations.

The business plan format normally consists of four parts: the introduction, the business concept, the financial plan, and the appendix.

The plan starts with an introductory page highlighting the business plan. Even though your entire business is described later, a crisp one- or two-page introduction helps capture the immediate attention of the potential investor or lender.

The business concept, which begins with a description of the industry, identifies your market potential within your industry and outlines your action plan for the coming year. Make sure your stated business goals are compatible with your personal goals and financial goals, your management ability, and family considerations. The heart of the business concept is your monthly sales forecast for the coming year. As your statement of confidence in your marketing strategy, it forms the basis for your cash flow forecast and projected income statement. This section also contains an assessment of business risks and a contingency plan. Being honest about your business risks and how you plan to deal with them is evidence of sound management.

The financial plan outlines the level of present financing and identifies the financing sought. This section should be brief. The financial plan contains financial forecasts. These forecasts are a projection into the future based on current information and assumptions. In carrying out your action plan for the coming year, these operating forecasts are an essential guide to business survival and profitability. It is important to refer to them often and, if circumstances dictate, rework them. Samples 5, 6, and 7 show forms you might want to include in your business plan.

The appendix section contains all the items that do not naturally fall elsewhere in the document, or which expand further on the summaries in the document. These might include a personal net worth statement (Sample 8) and a statement of accounts receivable (Sample 9).

ESTIMATING YOUR START-UP FUNDS

Assessment of personal monthly financial needs

Personal expenses will continue in spite of the business and have to be taken into account when determining monthly cash flow needs. It is important to calculate personal expenses accurately so that appropriate decisions can be made in terms of funding and the nature of the start-up practice – whether it should start out on a part-time or full-time basis, using the home as an office or renting an outside office. Refer back to Samples 2 and 3 in chapter 3 to review this important information.

Estimated business start-up cash needs

During your first few months you will probably not have enough sales revenue to finance your short-term costs. This usually occurs for one of three reasons: your sales are below projection, your costs rise unexpectedly, or you have not yet been paid for consulting work already performed (overdue accounts receivable). Many professionals experience accounts receivable problems during the early months of operation because clients tend to pay professionals after they have paid other outstanding bills. Your conservative cash flow analysis prepares you for this situation and enables you to plan your cash needs.

SUMMARY

Before presenting your business plan to a lender or investor, have two or three impartial outsiders review the finished plan in detail. There may be something you overlooked or underemphasized. After your plan has been reviewed by others, take it and your financial statements to your accountant for review. You should also discuss with your accountant all the personal and business tax considerations that might be involved. You may wish to have your accountant come with you to the bank when you discuss your loan proposal. This is not uncommon and can create a very positive impression.

Discuss with your solicitor the security you are proposing. Your solicitor should explain fully before the plan is submitted the effect of your pledging security and what the lender could do if you default. You should also seriously evaluate whether the security pledged is too excessive for the loan or risk involved and whether the risk is too great to pledge your personal assets.

Your familiarity with your business plan will increase your credibility and at the same time provide you with a good understanding of what the financial statements reveal about the viability of your business.

SAMPLE 4

BUSINESS PLAN FORMAT

1. Introductory page
   - (a) Company name
     - Include address and telephone number
   - (b) Contact person
     - Consultant's name and telephone number
   - (c) Paragraph about company
     - Nature of business and market area
   - (d) Securities offered to investors or lenders
     - Outline securities such as preferred shares, common shares, debentures, etc.
   - (e) Business loans sought
     - For example, term loan, operating line of credit, mortgage
   - (f) Summary of proposed use of funds
2. Summary
   - (a) Highlights of business plan
     - Preferably one page maximum
     - Include your project, competitive advantage, and "bottom line" needs
3. Table of contents
   - (a) Section titles and page numbers should be given for easy reference
4. Description of consultancy
   - (a) Outlook and growth potential
     - Outline industry trends – past, present, and future – and new developments
     - State your sources of information
   - (b) Markets and customers
     - Estimated size of total market, share and sales, new requirements, and market trends
   - (c) Competitive companies
     - Market share, strengths and weaknesses, profitability, trends
   - (d) National and economic trends
     - Population shifts, consumer trends, relevant economic indicators
5. Description of business venture
   - (a) Nature of consulting service
     - Characteristics, method of operation, whether performed locally, regionally, nationally, or internationally
   - (b) Target market
     - Typical clients identified by groups, present consulting patterns and average earnings, wants and needs
   - (c) Competitive advantage of your business concept
     - Your market niche, uniqueness, estimated market share

SAMPLE 4 (Continued)

    (d)   Business location and size
- Location relative to market, size of premises, home or office use

    (e)   Staff and equipment needed
- Overall requirement, capacity, home or office use, part- or full-time staff or as required

    (f)   Brief history
- Principals involved in the consulting business or proposed consulting business, development work done, CVs and background experience of principals, CVs of key consulting associates if applicable

6. Business goals

    (a)   One year
- Specific goals, such as utilization rates, fee income, profit margin, share of market, opening new office, introducing new service, etc.

    (b)   Over the longer term
- Return on investment, business net worth, sale of business

7. Marketing plan

    (a)   Sales strategy
- Sales objectives, sales media, sales support
- Target clients

    (b)   Sales approach
- Style of operation and techniques

    (c)   Pricing
- Costing, mark-ups, margins, break-even

    (d)   Promotion
- Media advertising, promotions, publicity appropriate to reach target market
- Techniques of developing exposure, credibility, and contacts

    (e)   Service policies
- Policies that your consulting practice will adopt with regard to credit and collection, bidding, nature of clients, etc.

    (f)   Guarantees
- Service performance guarantees or other assurances will vary depending upon nature of consulting practice and type of contract or client

    (g)   Tracking methods
- Method for confirming who your clients are and how they heard about you

8. Sales forecast

    (a)   Assumptions
- One never has all the necessary information, so state all the assumptions made in developing the forecast

SAMPLE 4 (*Continued*)

(b) Monthly forecast for the coming year
   – Sales volume, projected in £

(c) Annual forecast for the following two to four years
   – Sales volume, projected in £

The sales forecast is the starting point for your projected income statement and cash flow forecast.

9. Costing plan

   (a) Cost of facilities, equipment, and materials (as applicable)
      – Estimates and quotations

   (b) Capital estimates
      – One time start-up or expansion capital required

10. Operations

   (a) Purchasing plans

   (b) Space required
      – Floor and office space, improvements required, expansion capability

   (c) Staff and equipment required
      – Personnel by skill level
      – Fixtures, office equipment

   (d) Operations strategy

11. Corporate structure

   (a) Legal form
      – Sole trader, partnership, or limited company

   (b) Share distribution
      – List of principal shareholders

   (c) Contracts and agreements
      – List of contracts and agreements in force
      – Management contract, shareholder or partnership agreement, service contract, leases

   (d) Directors and officers
      – Names and addresses, role in company

   (e) Background of key management personnel
      – Brief CVs of active owners and key employees

   (f) Organizational chart
      – Identify reporting relationships

   (g) Duties and responsibilities of key personnel
      – Brief job descriptions – who is responsible for what

12. Supporting professional assistance

   (a) Professionals on contract in specialized or deficient areas; would include solicitor, accountant, bank manager, insurance agent, etc.

13. Research and development programme

SAMPLE 4 (Continued)

(a) Product or service improvements, process improvements, costs and risks

14. Risk assessment

   (a) Competitors' reaction
      - Will competitors try to squeeze you out? What form do you anticipate any reaction will take?

   (b) List of critical external factors that might occur
      - Identify effects of strikes, recession, new technology, new competition, shifts in consumer demand, costs of delays and overruns, unfavourable industry trends

   (c) List of critical internal factors that might occur
      - Income projections not realized, client dispute or litigation, receivables difficulties, demand for service increases very quickly, key employee or consultant quits

   (d) Dealing with risks
      - Contingency plan to handle the most significant risks

15. Overall schedule

   (a) Interrelationship and timing of all major events important to starting and developing your business

16. Action plan

   (a) Steps to accomplish this year's goals
      - Flow chart by month or by quarter of specific action to be taken and by whom

   (b) Checkpoint for measuring results
      - Identify significant dates, sales levels as decision points

17. Financial forecast

   If a business has been in operation for a period of time, the previous two or three years' balance sheets and income statements are required

   (a) Opening balance sheet
      - The balance sheet is a position statement, not an historical record; it shows what is owned and owed at a given date. There are three sections to a balance sheet: assets, liabilities, and owner's equity. You determine your firm's net worth by subtracting the liabilities from the assets.
      - Your balance sheet will indicate how your investment has grown over a period of time – investors and lenders typically examine balance sheets to determine if the company is within acceptable assets to liability limits
      - See Sample 5

   (b) Profit and loss forecast (budget)

SAMPLE 4 *(Continued)*

- The profit and loss forecast (budget) can be described as the operating statement you would expect to see for your business at the end of the period for which the forecast is being prepared
- For a new business, the budget would show what revenue and expenses you expect the business to have in its first year of operation
- It is very useful, of course, to prepare a forecast for a period longer than one year, so you might want to prepare a detailed budget for the next year of operation and a less detailed budget for the following two years
- Preparing an income and expense budget for a new business is more difficult than preparing one for an existing business, simply because in a new business there is no historical record to go by. For this reason the preparation of the forecast is an even more essential, interesting, and rewarding experience than doing it for an existing business, despite the time and effort required. This analysis exercise will answer the question of whether a profit will be made.
- The income statement (sales) is the most difficult because it is the most uncertain at the commencement of business; it is essential that a figure be projected on a conservative estimate
- The main concern is to account for expenses accurately and in as much detail as possible; this will then provide a target or break-even figure toward which to work
- Some headings may not be appropriate for your type of consulting practice; other headings should be added
- See Sample 6

(c) Cash flow forecast
- A cash flow budget measures the flow of money in and out of the business. It is critical to you and your bank.
- Many businesses operate on a seasonal basis, as there are slow months and busy months. The cash flow budget projection will provide an indication of the times of a cash flow shortage to assist in properly planning and financing your operation. It will tell you in advance if you have enough cash to get by.
- A cash flow budget should be prepared a year in advance and contain monthly breakdowns
- See Sample 7

(d) Cash flow assumptions
When reviewing the cash flow plan, certain assumptions should be made:
- Sales: monthly sales (consulting service fees) that are expected to materialize
- Receipts: cash sales represent cash actually received

SAMPLE 4 (*Continued*)

- Disbursements: accounts payable to be paid in month following month of purchase
- Accounting and legal: to be paid upon receipt of bill, expected to be in the spring or after your trading year end financial statements have been completed
- Advertising: anticipated to be the same amount each month and paid for in the month the expense is incurred
- Car expenses: anticipated to be the same amount each month and paid for in the month the expense is incurred
- Bank charges and interest: anticipated to be the same amount each month and paid for in the month the expense is incurred
- Equipment rental: to be paid for in monthly payments
- Income taxes: amount for taxes of the previous year and to be paid in the current year
- Insurance: annual premium to be paid quarterly, semi-annually, or annually in instalments of equal amounts
- Loan repayment: amount is the same each month and paid in accordance with the monthly schedule furnished by the lending institution
- Office supplies and expenses: to be paid in month following receipt of invoice and supplies to be purchased on a quarterly basis
- Taxes and licences: to be paid for upon receipt of invoice
- Telephone: to be paid for monthly or quarterly
- Utilities: expected to fluctuate seasonally and to be paid quarterly
- Salaries and benefits: amount considered to be the same each month and paid for in the month the expense is incurred
- Miscellaneous: expected to be the same each month and paid for in the month the expense is incurred
- Bad debts: varies

(e) Break-even analysis

- The break-even analysis is a critical calculation for every consulting business. Rather than calculating how much your firm would make if it attained an estimated sales volume, a more meaningful analysis determines at what sales volume your firm will break even. An estimated sales volume could be very unreliable as there are many factors which could affect revenue. Above the break-even sales volume it is only a matter of how much money your business can generate; below the break-even level of sales, it is only a matter of how many days a business can operate before bankruptcy.
- A break-even analysis provides a very real and meaningful figure to work toward; you may need to update it every few months to reflect your business growth
- The break-even point is where total costs are equal to total revenues

SAMPLE 4 (Continued)

- The calculation of total costs is determined by adding variable costs onto the fixed costs
- Total costs are all costs of operating the business over a specified time period
- Variable costs are those that vary directly with the number of consulting services provided or marketing and promotion activities undertaken. These typically include car expenses, business travel expenses, supplies, brochures, etc. Variable costs are not direct costs which are passed on to the client in invoicing.
- Fixed costs are costs that do not generally vary with the number of clients serviced. Also known as indirect costs, these costs typically include salaries, rent, secretarial services, insurance, telephone, accounting and legal supplies.

18. Financing and capitalization
    (a) Loan applied for
        - The amount, terms, and when required
    (b) Purpose of loan
        - Attach a detailed description of the aspects of the business to be financed
    (c) Owner's equity
        - The amount of your financial commitment to the business
    (d) Summary of loan requirements
        - For a particular consulting project or for the business as a whole

19. Operating loan
    (a) Overdraft facility applied for
        - A new overdraft or an increase, and security offered if necessary
    (b) Maximum operating cash required
        - Amount required, timing of need (refer to "cash flow forecast")

20. Present financing (if applicable)
    (a) Loans outstanding
        - The balance owing, repayment terms, purpose, security, and status
    (b) Current operating line of credit
        - The amount and security held

21. References
    (a) Name of current lending institution
        - Branch and type of accounts
    (b) Solicitor's name
        - Solicitor's address and telephone number
    (c) Accountant's name
        - Accountant's address and telephone number

SAMPLE 4 (*Continued*)

22. Appendix

      The nature of the contents of the appendixes attached, if any, depends on the circumstances and requirements of the lender or investor, or the desire to enhance the loan proposal. It is recommended that the appendices be prepared for your own benefit and reference to assist your business analysis, and to be available if the information is required. The following list is a guide only. Some of the headings described may be unavailable or unnecessary.

    (a)   Personal net worth statement

         – Includes personal property values, investments, cash, bank loans, charge accounts, mortgages, and other liabilities. This will substantiate the value of your personal guarantee if required for security

         – See Sample 8

    (b)   Letter of intent

         – Potential orders for client commitments

    (c)   Description of personal and business insurance coverage

         – Include insurance policies and amount of coverage

    (d)   Accounts receivable summary

         – Include schedule

         – See Sample 9

    (e)   Accounts payable summary

         – Include a schedule of payments and total amounts owing

    (f)   Legal agreements

         – Include a copy of contracts, leases, and other documents

    (g)   Appraisals

         – Fair market value of business property and equipment

    (h)   Financial statements for associated companies

         – Where appropriate, a lender may require this information

    (i)   Copies of your brochure

    (j)   Testimonial letters from clients

    (k)   References

    (l)   Sales forecast and market surveys

    (m) List of investors

    (n)   Credit status information

    (o)   News articles about you and your business

SAMPLE 5

OPENING BALANCE SHEET (NEW BUSINESS)

DATE: _____ NAME OF COMPANY: _____

ASSETS

Current assets

    Cash and bank accounts   £ _____

    Accounts receivable   £ _____

    Inventory   £ _____

    Prepaid rent   £ _____

    Other current assets   £ _____

TOTAL CURRENT ASSETS   (A) £ _____

Fixed assets

    Land and buildings   £ _____

    Furniture, fixtures, and equipment   £ _____

    Cars   £ _____

    Leasehold improvements   £ _____

    Other assets   £ _____

TOTAL FIXED AND OTHER ASSETS   (B) £ _____

TOTAL ASSETS (A + B = C)   (C) £ _____

LIABILITIES

Current liabilities (debt due within next 12 months)

Bank loans   £ _____

Loans – other   £ _____

Accounts payable   £ _____

Current portion of long-term debt   £ _____

Other current liabilities   £ _____

TOTAL CURRENT LIABILITIES   (D) £ _____

Long-term debt   £ _____

Mortgages and liens payable (attach details)   £ _____

Less: current portion   £ _____

Loans from partners or stockholders (owner's equity)   £ _____

Other loans of long-term nature   £ _____

TOTAL LONG-TERM DEBT   (E) £ _____

TOTAL LIABILITIES (D + E = F)   (F) £ _____

NET WORTH (C – F = G)   (G) £ _____

TOTAL NET WORTH AND LIABILITIES (F + G = H)   (H) £ _____

SAMPLE 6

INCOME AND EXPENSE STATEMENT FORECAST (NEW BUSINESS)

(Name of business)

For the period: _____ **months ending** _____, **20** _____

PROJECTED INCOME

    SALES

        _____ £ _____

        _____ £ _____

    TOTAL SALES   £ _____

    OTHER INCOME   £ _____

TOTAL INCOME   (A) £ _____

PROJECTED EXPENSES

    SALES EXPENSES

      Salaries   £ _____

      Travel   £ _____

      Advertising   £ _____

      Automotive   £ _____

      Other   £ _____

TOTAL SELLING EXPENSES   (B) £ _____

ADMINISTRATIVE AND FINANCIAL EXPENSES

    Management salaries (or proprietor/partner draws)   £ _____

    Office salaries   £ _____

    Professional fees   £ _____

    Office expense and supplies   £ _____

    Telephone   £ _____

    Rent   £ _____

    Interest and bank charges   £ _____

    Inventory   £ _____

    Bad debt   £ _____

    Other   £ _____

TOTAL ADMINISTRATIVE AND FINANCIAL EXPENSES   (C) £ _____

TOTAL EXPENSES (B + C = D)   (D) £ _____

OPERATING PROFIT (LOSS) (A – D)   £ _____

Add: Other income   £ _____

Less: Provisions for income taxes   £ _____

NET PROFIT (LOSS)   £ _____

SAMPLE 7

CASH FLOW BUDGET WORKSHEET

	JANUARY Estimated	JANUARY Actual	FEBRUARY Estimated	FEBRUARY Actual	MARCH Estimated	MARCH Actual
Cash at beginning of month:						
In bank and on hand	£_____	£_____	£_____	£_____	£_____	£_____
In investments	£_____	£_____	£_____	£_____	£_____	£_____
TOTAL CASH	£_____	£_____	£_____	£_____	£_____	£_____
Plus income during month:						
Credit sales payments	_____	_____	_____	_____	_____	_____
Investment income	_____	_____	_____	_____	_____	_____
Receivables collected	_____	_____	_____	_____	_____	_____
Loans	_____	_____	_____	_____	_____	_____
Personal investment	_____	_____	_____	_____	_____	_____
Other cash income	_____	_____	_____	_____	_____	_____
TOTAL CASH AND INCOME	£_____	£_____	£_____	£_____	£_____	£_____
Expenses during the month:						
Rent (if applicable)	_____	_____	_____	_____	_____	_____
Utilities	_____	_____	_____	_____	_____	_____
Phone	_____	_____	_____	_____	_____	_____
Postage	_____	_____	_____	_____	_____	_____
Office equipment and furniture	_____	_____	_____	_____	_____	_____
Stationery and business cards	_____	_____	_____	_____	_____	_____
Insurance (health, fire, liability, theft, etc.)	_____	_____	_____	_____	_____	_____
Answering service	_____	_____	_____	_____	_____	_____

SAMPLE 7 (Continued)

Printing and supplies	_____	_____	_____	_____
Typing/secretarial service	_____	_____	_____	_____
Accounting and legal services	_____	_____	_____	_____
Advertising and promotion	_____	_____	_____	_____
Business licences and permits	_____	_____	_____	_____
Dues and subscriptions	_____	_____	_____	_____
Books and reference materials	_____	_____	_____	_____
Travel: in town	_____	_____	_____	_____
Travel: out of town	_____	_____	_____	_____
Conferences, professional meetings, trade shows	_____	_____	_____	_____
Continuing professional development	_____	_____	_____	_____
Entertainment	_____	_____	_____	_____
Contributions	_____	_____	_____	_____
Gifts	_____	_____	_____	_____
Salaries	_____	_____	_____	_____
Unemployment insurance	_____	_____	_____	_____
Pensions	_____	_____	_____	_____
Miscellaneous	_____	_____	_____	_____
Loan repayment	_____	_____	_____	_____
Other cash expenses	_____	_____	_____	_____
TOTAL EXPENSES	£_____	£_____	£_____	£_____
Cash flow excess (deficit) at end of month	£_____	£_____	£_____	£_____
Cash flow cumulative (monthly)	£_____	£_____	£_____	£_____

SAMPLE 8

PERSONAL NET WORTH STATEMENT

Date: _____

Name: _____

Address: _____

GENERAL INFORMATION

Phone: Home _____ Business _____ Age _____

Dependants including spouse _____

Present employer _____

Position occupied _____

How long with this employer _____

Previous employer _____ How long _____

Housing status, eg, owner occupier, tenant

Address _____

Monthly rent £ _____

Salary, wages or commission per annum £ _____

Other income per annum £ _____

Source _____

Guarantees on debts of others:

Name _____ Amount _____

Name _____ Amount _____

ASSETS

Bank accounts _____

Stocks at cost (market value_____) _____

Bonds at cost (market value_____) _____

Life insurance (cash surrender value) _____

      Beneficiary _____

Car: year _____ make _____ _____

Home _____

Other significant assets _____

                                      TOTAL _____

LIABILITIES

Bank loan _____

Charge accounts _____

Policy loans on life insurance _____

Other loans _____

Instalment purchases _____

Mortgages: Interest rate _____

Term _____ Payments _____ _____

Taxes _____

Other liabilities _____

      SUB TOTAL _____

NET WORTH _____

      TOTAL _____

(Name of company)

SAMPLE 9

STATEMENT OF ACCOUNTS RECEIVABLE

AS AT _____ 20 ____

Date: _____

(Name of company)

Names of debtors	Total Days	Current Days	31–60	61–90	Over 90 Days & Holdbacks	Remarks

1. Sub totals £ _____

2. Aggregate of accounts
   under £ _____ £ _____

3. Number of
   accounts   No. _____   No. _____   No. _____   No. _____   No. _____

4. TOTALS £   _____
   Percentage   _____ 100%   %   %   %   %

7

How to obtain financing

Having completed your business plan and financial projections, you should now have a clear idea of your short-term and medium-term financial needs. You will want to be familiar with the types of financing available, the various sources, how to approach financial lending institutions, and the type of security that may be required. You should also be aware of the reasons that lending institutions or investors may turn down a request for funding. These matters and other issues are covered in this chapter.

TYPES OF FINANCING

There are two basic types of financing: equity and debt.

Equity

The money that you put into a company or business is equity. Initially all money must come from your own resources such as savings or personal borrowing from financial institutions, friends, relatives, or business associates. As time progresses, retained earnings in the business will increase your equity.

Debt

A debt is a loan. It must be repaid, and the lender will charge interest on the money you have borrowed. With borrowed money, normally the principal with interest is paid back on a fixed monthly payment. You therefore have to include the principal and interest payments in a current business plan. Various forms of debt financing are discussed below.

Short-term or operating loan (demand loan)

Short-term or operating loans are used for financing inventory, accounts receivable, special purchases or promotions, and other items requiring working capital during peak periods.

The main sources of short-term loans are commercial banks or similar financial institutions. Using a short-term loan is a good way to establish credit with a bank. This type of loan can be unsecured or secured by your personal or business assets.

Short-term loans are usually negotiated for specific periods of time; for example, 30, 60, or 90 days and frequently for periods of up to a year or more. They may be repayable in a lump sum at the end of the period or in periodic instalments, such as monthly.

Other characteristics of a demand loan include:

▌ The interest rate at time of signing may be lower than for a term loan.

▌ There is a fluctuating interest rate.

▌ Repayment of the loan can be demanded at any time by the lender; this usually only occurs when the account does not perform satisfactorily or in case of serious deterioration in the affairs of the business.

▌ A short-term loan can often be obtained more quickly than a longer-term loan.

Overdraft

Overdrafts are usually subject to annual review and renewal. Other characteristics of an overdraft include:

▌ Loan funds increase and decrease as you use the money or make deposits. This is referred to as a revolving line of credit.

▌ They are available from most banks.

▌ There is a fluctuating interest rate.

▌ The interest rate at time of signing may be lower than for a loan.

▌ The lender uses accounts receivable (the money owed to you by customers) and inventory as the security. For accounts receivable, the lender may lend between 50% and 75% of the value, not including amounts over 90 days. For inventory, a lender may lend up to 50%.

▌ An overdraft can often be obtained more quickly than a loan.

▌ Repayment of the loan can be demanded at any time by the lender or the overdraft can be reduced; usually this only occurs when the account does not perform satisfactorily or in a case of serious deterioration in the affairs of the business, or reduction in the value of the security provided.

▌ The size of an overdraft is based on the lender's assessment of the creditworthiness of the company, its principals, and the credit requested, among other factors.

Loans

A loan is generally money borrowed for a term of from 1 to 15 years. The regular loan payments include principal and interest and are for a fixed aggregate amount over the life or term of the loan agreement.

Loans are commonly used to provide funds for the purchase of an existing business, to help finance expansions or capital expenditures, and to provide additional working capital for a growing business.

While the majority of loans are secured by collateral such as fixed assets or other chattels (cars, building, land, equipment, etc), the lender places great importance on the ability of the borrower to repay his or her indebtedness out of the business's earnings over the life of the loan.

The main characteristics of a loan are:

▌ It may be repaid over a period of time generally related to the useful 'life' of the assets; for example, car – three to five years; land and building – after three years.

▌ The lender will only give you a percentage of the value; for example, car – 80%; building – 75%. The other 20% or 25% of the cost of the asset must come from the equity you have in the company or new funds from shareholders or yourself.

▌ The company must be able to show the lender that future sales will generate enough cash to repay the loan.

▌ There are different lenders for different types of loans. One consideration in the approval of your proposal is 'leverage' or 'debt to equity ratio'. This is the ratio of the money you owe to the money you put in the business. Generally, the lender's assessment of this ratio is discretionary, but if you are a new business, or just building up a reputation, it is unlikely that the lender will want to go beyond 2:1 or even 1:1. Consequently, this may place an additional restriction on the amount that you can borrow.

▌ Interest rate at time of signing is slightly higher than for a demand loan.

▌ Your payments, principal plus interest, are all the same.

▌ Repayment period of loan is specified and agreed upon in advance.

Trade credit or supplier financing

This is the most often used form of short-term financing. This means that a supplier will not insist on immediate payment for purchase of merchandise.

Terms of payment – generally 30 to 90 days – can be arranged between both parties.

Renting or leasing

Renting or leasing assets is an alternative form of financing. Leasing companies will consider arranging a lease with an option to purchase on virtually any tangible asset. Renting premises, as opposed to buying a building, is also a financing alternative. Typewriters, office furniture, computers, cars, and telephone equipment are examples of assets that can be leased or rented. The advantages of leasing are:

▌ It frees up equity capital for investment in areas of greater return.

▌ It frees up borrowing power for the more critical areas of the business.

▌ There is no down payment requirement with leasing.

▌ Rates are usually fixed for a set term.

▌ The full payment is an allowable expense.

▌ Purchase options can be exercised at a later date at a predetermined price.

There are also disadvantages. You should discuss the tax and financial considerations with your accountant before you make your decision.

SOURCES OF FINANCING

Equity

The most common source of equity capital is personal funds from savings. In exchange for the funds provided to the company, the owner obtains all the shares of the company or ownership of the business.

Equity can be further increased from the savings of friends willing to invest, or even from relatives. However, many small business people have created problems by bringing in friends or relatives as investors.

Conflicts generally occur if the business is not doing as well as everyone initially imagined, or if the terms and conditions of such loans are not clearly spelled out, or if the lenders or investors insist on becoming involved in day-to-day operations.

Any agreement should be documented in writing between the parties and signed in advance to eliminate any misunderstanding. Agreement should be reached on the rate of interest to be paid, when the loans will be repaid, any options you have to pay them back early, and the procedures that all parties will follow if the loans become delinquent. Consult competent legal counsel in advance to protect your interests.

An equity investment can be in the form of stockholder loans, or common stock or shares in the company, or a combination of loans and shares. The investment structure will vary in each situation.

Generally, the advantage of money being invested as shareholder loans is that it can be paid back to lenders without tax, other than personal tax and interest you receive before the loan is paid off.

If the money is in the form of shares, it is much more difficult to withdraw since shares must be sold to someone else and may be subject to capital gains tax.

Long-term debt investors may therefore place restrictions or conditions on when and how the company can pay off shareholder loans, redeem shares, or possibly even pay dividends on shares. These restrictions or conditions are imposed to protect the long-term debt invested.

The advice of a tax accountant is recommended since your personal tax situation and that of other potential equity investors could have a bearing on whether the shareholder investment should be in the form of loans or purchase of shares.

Debt

Commercial banks are a major source of capital for new and continuing small ventures. Additional organizations that provide financing include insurance companies, pension companies, property companies, venture capital companies, banks, and even trust companies and credit unions.

COMPETITION BETWEEN LENDERS

There is considerable competition among banks and other financial institutions. Compare at least three different financial institutions to assess the most favourable loan package available.

All aspects of financial dealings are negotiable. Obtain the lending terms in writing before you sign. Have your outside advisers, such as your accountant or solicitor, review the terms. In addition, you may want to obtain the advice of your associates. Don't rush into a relationship with a financial institution without reasonably exploring all the other alternatives.

TIPS ON APPROACHING YOUR LENDER

When you approach a financial institution, you must sell the merits of your business proposal. As in all sales presentations, consider the needs and expectations of the other party. The institution's managers will be interested in the following:

(a) Your familiarity with the business concept and the realities of the marketplace as reflected in your detailed business plan.

(b) Your ability to service the debt with sufficient surplus to cover contingencies, including carrying interest charges, and eventually repay the debt in full as demonstrated in your cash flow forecast and projected income statement.

(c) Your level of commitment as shown by your equity in the business or cash investment in the particular asset being purchased.

(d) Your secondary source of repayment, including security in the event of default, and other sources of income.

(e) Your track record and integrity as shown in your personal credit history, your business plan, and business results or past business experience.

(f) Your approach. During the loan interview remember you're doing business just as you do when you're with a client. Don't be subservient, overly familiar, or too aggressive. Keep in mind that a lender is in business for the same reason you are – to make a profit. Keep the profit motive in mind during the interview. Don't try to appeal to a lender's social conscience. It won't work, since loans aren't granted for their social impact.

(g) Your judgement in supplying information. Be sensible about the number of documents you provide at the outset. You do not want to overwhelm people with too much material. For example, the introductory page, summary, and financial plan sections provide a good basic loan submission if the amount requested is small. You should have all other documents prepared and available if requested.

(h) Your personal appearance. You should present yourself in a manner that projects self-confidence and success.

(i) Your mental alertness. What time during the day are you at your mental peak? This should be the time that you arrange an interview.

(j) Your consideration in allowing sufficient lead time for approval. The lender needs a reasonable time to assess your proposal. Also, the loan may have to be referred to another level within the financial institution for review.

(k) Your credit rating. It's a good idea to review your credit rating periodically, as there may be errors to correct in your file. Note your positive and negative points so you can discuss them when they are raised by the lender.

If your request for financing is approved, find out everything you need to know about the conditions, terms, payment methods, interest rates, security requirements, and any other fees to be paid. No commitment to accept the financing should be made until all this information is provided and understood and its impact on the proposed business analysed. Ask your accountant and solicitor to assist you in the loan application in advance and review the bank's approval. Make certain you get the approval particulars in writing.

WHY LOANS ARE TURNED DOWN

If a request for financing is not approved, find out why. Use the lender's experience to your advantage. Lenders handle many requests for financing and have experience in the financial aspects of many businesses, even if they do not have direct management experience.

If there is something specifically wrong with the financing proposal, see if it can be corrected and then reapply. If not, use this knowledge when approaching other potential lenders or on future occasions when seeking funds.

A loan could be rejected for the following reasons:

(a) The business idea was considered unsound or too risky. A lender's judgement is generally based on past performance of other businesses similar to the one you are proposing.

(b) Insufficient collateral. A lender must be satisfied that there are sufficient assets pledged to meet the outstanding debt if your business does not succeed financially. If you are just starting a business, a lender generally requires you to pledge personal assets, such as your home, car, and other securities, against the loan. If you are borrowing funds under a company name, your personal guarantee will generally be requested and in some cases your spouse's guarantee as well, depending on the circumstances. You may therefore not have sufficient security required for the amount of loan you are requesting or for the degree of risk, in the lender's opinion, that might be involved.

(c) Lack of financial commitment on your part. A lender will be reluctant to approve loan financing for business ventures if you are not fully committed. The lender does not want to foreclose or repossess and then have to sell assets to collect your money. The lender will therefore want to know how much personal financial capital you have made available to the business venture in order to assess your commitment to repay the loan. If you have not made any financial commitment and yet have security that you wish to pledge, the security alone may not be sufficient.

(d) Lack of a business plan or a poor business plan. A lender could reject your loan application if you have not prepared a detailed business plan or do not understand its significance.

(e) The purpose of the loan is not explained or is not acceptable. It is important that the specific use of the funds being borrowed be outlined in detail. It is also important that the purpose and amount of funds being requested be reasonable and appropriate. For example, it could be considered unreasonable for you to calculate a large draw or salary from your business in the first six months. If you intend to use the loan to pay off past debts or financial obligations, it may not be approved since the funds would not be directly generating cash flow for your new business venture.

(f) Your character, personality, or stability can affect a lender's decision. It is important to appear confident, enthusiastic, well informed, and realistic. If your personality is not consistent with the personality required for your type of business in the eyes of the lender, it could have a negative effect. If you are going through a separation or divorce proceedings or have declared personal bankruptcy or had business failures in the past, these factors could have an adverse impact on your loan application.

8

Keeping records

A consultant must keep accurate and thorough financial records covering all income received and expenses incurred. Records help in producing income, controlling expenses, planning growth and cash flow, keeping tax payments to a legal minimum, and complying with regulatory requirements. This chapter explains the basic concepts and procedures of keeping records and outlines some of the issues you will have to discuss with your accountant and bookkeeper.

ACCOUNTING AND BOOKKEEPING

Accounting is the process of analysing and systematically recording, in terms of money or some other unit of measurement, operations or transactions of the business. To capture these facts and figures, a system is necessary. Such a system usually consists of bookkeeping records that may be set up in journals, ledgers, or other records.

A professional accountant can help design a system for recording the information each consultant needs in his or her particular circumstance. Some tips on selecting an accountant are outlined in chapter 5.

Bookkeeping is the process of classifying and recording business transactions in the books of account. A bookkeeper keeps the various records, journals, and ledgers current and accurate.

Many consultants are not inclined or do not know how to maintain the books. A part-time bookkeeper can be employed to keep the books either at your home or place of business, or at the bookkeeper's office. It is highly advisable that a professional accountant establish a system for your books. You can then hire a bookkeeper recommended by your accountant or by a business associate you trust.

Make sure the bookkeeper is competent to handle your specific type of records, as some bookkeepers specialize in certain areas. The costs of a bookkeeper are considerably lower than those for a professional accountant, but bookkeepers are not qualified to provide tax advice. Only an experienced tax accountant is able to provide you with the necessary tax planning information.

Different kinds of bookkeeping systems are discussed below.

Separate record-keeping

It is essential that your business books and records be kept separate from your personal books, records, and bank accounts. This is sound business management. Separate records will allow you to control cash flow, budget for expenses, and draw up financial statements. A separate bank account for the business has the following advantages:

▌ Financial statements can be drawn and taxable income computed easily.

▌ When all income is deposited into the business account, the income journal is maintained by the bank in the form of complete records of all receipts.

▌ Applications for financing for business purposes can be prepared more accurately with business account records.

▌ All business expenses can be proven from one source.

▌ Personal drawings from the business can be budgeted carefully and completely controlled. Funds can be taken from the business account periodically and deposited into the personal account as drawings or salary.

Double-entry and single-entry bookkeeping

Double-entry bookkeeping is usually the preferred method for keeping business records. Transactions are entered first in a journal, then monthly totals of the transactions are posted to the appropriate ledger accounts. The ledger accounts include five categories: income, expense, asset, liability, and net worth. Income and expense accounts are closed each year; asset, liability, and net worth accounts are maintained on a permanent and continuing basis.

Single-entry bookkeeping is not as complete as a double-entry method. This system, however, is relatively simple and records the flow of income and expense through a daily summary of cash receipts, a monthly summary of receipts, and a monthly disbursements journal, such as a cheque book.

Your accountant will advise you about the appropriate system for your needs.

Computer software

There are many accounting and bookkeeping software programs available in the marketplace. Most have spreadsheets or are spreadsheet compatible. Ask your colleagues and accountant which programs they recommend and why. Comparison shop for the features and benefits that meet your current and projected needs.

BASIC ACCOUNTING RECORDS

As previously discussed, informal records consist of evidence of business transactions such as sales slips, invoices, cheques, etc. These informal records are then gathered into a more formal structure. For accounting purposes, these formalized basic records are referred to as 'books of original entries' or as 'journals.'

Sales journal

A sales journal is a daily register of both cash and charge sales. The sales, both cash and charge, may be recorded by numbered invoices and accounted for. The total is then entered as the day's sales in the sales journal.

Cash receipts journal

This journal often combines the function of a sales journal along with a record of all transactions resulting in money coming into the business. When combined, this journal is referred to as a 'sales and cash receipts journal.'

In the cash receipts journal, all cash sales, charge sales, collections on account, and total deposits to the bank are entered. This is usually done in conjunction with the cash receipts journal. Referred to as a 'daily summary of sales and cash receipts,' it is both a summarizing vehicle and a form of reconciliation between cash on hand, cash receipts, charge sales, and total sales.

A sales and cash receipts journal briefly describes the transaction, whether it is a cash sale or a charge sale, whether the cash receipt came from a source other than a sale, and the amount of the total deposit.

In summary, the journal will show:

(a) Cash sale

(b) Bank deposit

(c) Receipts on account from a client

(d) Other receipts.

Accounts receivable ledger and control account

These records are separate. The accounts receivable ledger contains separate cards or sheets for each charge client and records the sale with the invoice number or reference, the date, and the amount of the sale. When payments are made, the amount of the payment is deducted from the balance owing and is cross-referenced to the cash receipts journal.

The control account records in total all the charge sales and all the payments by charge customers which are detailed individually in the accounts receivable ledger. At any given time, the sum of all the individual charge account balances in the subsidiary ledger will equal the total net balance in the control account. The accounts receivable ageing schedule accompanies the accounts receivable ledger. This is a record of each charge customer that shows the balance owing and the age status of the charge.

In summary, each client has a ledger sheet that details name, address, telephone number, credit information, date of sale, invoice number, date of payment, receipt number, balance owing.

Periodically the individual balances are added up (usually once a month), and the totals are reconciled to the accounts receivable balance in the general ledger.

Accounts payable journal

This journal is usually a subsidiary journal to the cash disbursements journal. The accounts payable journal records invoices for purchases, the amount and date, and when the invoice has to be paid. This journal's purpose is primarily a control over the payables. It allows you to correctly determine outstanding liabilities and when these obligations must be met.

Cash disbursements journal

This journal records daily all cash outlays for purchases, expenses, payroll, cash withdrawals, and loan payments. The payee or account is referenced, the cheque number is given, the amount is specified, and the purpose of the disbursement, by amount, is shown under the proper heading for each day. The purpose could be payroll, inventory purchased, accounts payable falling due, tax payments, etc. Any disbursements, such as interest charges or withdrawals, are also recorded.

Payroll journal

This journal consists usually of two records. The first is the record for the individual employee; it shows the pay period, the gross amount earned, the deductions (PAYE, National Insurance, pension contributions, etc) made at source, and the net earnings. The second record is the 'payroll summary' which, for the pay period, gives the total gross earnings, deductions, and net salaries paid to all employees. The total of the employees' salaries appears as an entry in the cash disbursements journal.

General ledger

The general ledger is the final book of entry in an accounting system. This record is required to complete even the most basic of bookkeeping systems. Every entry from the preceding journals and ledgers is listed in the general ledger. The general ledger must always be kept in balance; that is to say, all debits and credits must be equal, so that the net additions and subtractions equal zero. The general ledger is used to prepare financial statements. Because it is the book of final entry and a permanent record, none of the pages should ever be thrown away.

Tax records

Tax records record details of VAT, income taxes, corporation tax and business rates, and employee income tax deductions. The information is obtained from different aspects of the business operations. For example, payroll deductions and service are obtained from the payroll records, and information on VAT collected comes from either the sales journal or the daily summary of sales and cash receipts.

Tax records detail assessments, rates, calculations, and remittances both by amount and date. Tax records also let you know when remittances must be made to avoid late filing penalties.

Computer software for record-keeping

Most standard accounting software programs have the main bookkeeping record systems such as general ledger, accounts payable and receivable, ageing of accounts, payroll, cash, and sales. Check with your local software store for products that might meet your needs.

NONFINANCIAL RECORDS

Administrative records can improve efficiency and profit. Nonfinancial records such as personnel records and service records should be maintained.

Personnel records

Personnel records consist primarily of policies, benefits, and other matters pertaining to the general administration of the employees or consultants as a whole. Personnel records can also consist of individual records on each employee. These records contain all documents and correspondence relating to an employee from the time of applying for employment to termination. Individual employee records also include a summary of personal data, education and training, work history, and job and wage record.

Service records

Service records are all the records associated with the provision of a service. Most important, these records are used to record, for each client, the cost of material, labour, and overheads. These calculations are then used to determine a price when bidding on a contract or presenting a proposal, or assessing the profitability of a particular activity or product.

Service records can also keep track of employee efficiency to control nonchargeable time and to identify activities that are not performed to expected standards.

OFFICE SYSTEMS

Office systems should be implemented to reduce exposure to liability and to increase business awareness and sound decision-making.

Handling new clients and projects

It is important that a form be developed to gather administrative information in a standard, consistent, and uniform manner to reduce the likelihood of an error or omission. The form should provide date and deadlines, as well as information that might give rise to potential conflicts of interest. You should have separate forms for prospective clients and new assignments. See Samples 10 and 11.

Timesheet records

Maintenance of effective timesheets is critical in documenting what was done by the consultant or sub-consultant. Such records must be made as business is transacted.

Accurate timesheets are extremely important to ensure that clients are promptly charged and that you have accounted for all billable time expended. It is easy to forget time expended if you don't write it down immediately. Timesheets also reflect the expenditure of time for the benefit received, and whether or not your efficiency and profit are improving or certain activities or clients should be reconsidered. See Sample 12.

If there is a legal dispute, your timesheet and service documentation could make the difference between winning and losing. Keep your timesheets in a detailed fashion as if you had to introduce them as evidence into court. The odds are that at some point in your consulting career you will have to do so. Consider using a handheld device to help you keep a check on the time spent on a job. Carry it with you at all times and transfer all notations to your daily timesheet. You should get into the habit of recording all your daily activities in your daytimer, whether client related or not, so that you can graphically analyse how your time is spent. For example, make a note of hours spent each day on client entertainment, marketing, professional development, and research.

Standard form engagement letters or contracts

You should have your lawyer help you develop letters of agreement and contracts that you can modify for each particular situation. It is important that the services to be performed and fee to be rendered are clearly outlined in a written contract.

Invoicing, credit, and collection

Monthly or interim invoicing should be done whenever possible. This means invoices can be sent close to the time the work was done. It also keeps your cash flow even and enables you to spot fee disputes while there is still time to remedy the problem. An effective system can include a standard credit application form, client account record, etc. This subject is covered in detail in chapter 12.

Calendars

Important dates and deadlines should be entered into an effective calendar system that will provide a double-check on entries, adequate lead time for performance of tasks, deadlines, limitation dates, secretarial administration of the system, input by associates and sub-consultants as appropriate, and follow-up to ensure that the performance has occurred.

Filing systems

An effective filing system should be developed to eliminate the possibility of misplacement of client materials. A filing reference system should be designed for speedy retrieval of client information.

Computer systems

Manual systems provide efficient office management, but you may want to consider the benefits of a computer system. All the elements of a full accounting record can be retained on a computer database. This will save time and money. Automatic back-ups and off-site storage of data protect your records in case of system failure or a power surge. There are software programs available with time systems, standardized contracts, etc.

SAMPLE 10
PROSPECTIVE CLIENT SHEET

File no. _____

Telephone _____

Name _____

Address _____

_____

LEAD

Date of enquiry _____

Person making enquiry _____

Source of referral _____

Nature of initial enquiry _____

Consultant contacted _____

Follow-up planned _____

Dates of:

    Phone conversations _____

    Meetings _____

    Correspondence _____

Total time expended on client prior
    to any proposal preparation _____

Status _____

PROPOSAL

Presentation date of proposal _____

Time required to complete proposal _____

Cost estimate _____

Consultant with primary
    responsibility for assignment _____

ASSIGNMENT

Starting date _____

Consultant(s) assigned _____

Primary client contact _____

Total invoice _____

Completion date _____

SAMPLE 11

NEW CONSULTING ASSIGNMENT SHEET

File no. _____ Consultant in charge_____ New client ( )

Old client ( )

Client _____ Date opened_____

Address _____ Phone_____

Contact person(s) _____

Cross index _____

Assignment _____

Type of work:

( ) Feasibility study ( ) Marketing study ( ) Research

( ) Grant acquisition ( ) Organizational study ( ) Speaking engagement

( ) Management study ( ) Personnel/labour study ( ) Training

( ) Other

Fees (costs additional):

Person/Class	Rate	Per	Range quoted £	to £ _____
			Minimum quoted	£ _____
			Time value	£ _____

Other fee arrangements (method of payment) _____

Costs (projected) _____

Total fees and costs _____

Source of client contact _____

Promised completion date _____

Expected completion date _____

Opened by _____

CLOSING INFORMATION

Assignment completed on _____

Time value £ _____ Total fee rec'd £ _____ Variance £ _____

Client available for reference: Yes ( ) No ( )

SAMPLE 12

TIME AND SERVICE RECORD

Date	Client No.	Client Name	Service	Service Code	Loc'n Code	Time		By
						Hours	Decimal Conv.	

					TOTAL TIME:

Services codes | Local code

1 ADV Advice
2 AP Appear
3 AUD Audit
4 CON Conference
5 DIC Dictate
6 DR Draft

7 ENT Entertain
8 INT Interview
9 INV Investigate
10 OF Office
11 PR Promotion
12 RES Research

13 REV Review
14 SEC Secretarial
15 TCF Phone call from
16 TCT Phone call to
17 TVL Travel
18 TR Train

A In Town
B Out of Town
C Client's Office
D Other

Decimal Conversion:

6 minutes = .1 hour   36 minutes = .6 hour
12 minutes = .2 hour   42 minutes = .7 hour
18 minutes = .3 hour   48 minutes = .8 hour
24 minutes = .4 hour   54 minutes = .9 hour
30 minutes = .5 hour   60 minutes = 1.0 hour

9

Tax considerations

THINGS TO DO AT THE OUTSET

As soon as you start work on your own account, you or your accountant should tell your local Inspector of Taxes. The Inspector's address appears in the local telephone directory under 'Inland Revenue'.

If you have given up your previous employment, you should send your local Inspector of Taxes the form P45 given to you by your last employer when you left.

If you employ someone in the business, you may have to deduct income tax under PAYE arrangements (see later in this chapter).

If your taxable turnover exceeds certain limits, you must be registered for value added tax (VAT) (also dealt with later).

ACCOUNTING PERIODS

The first accounting period of a new business can be any period that you choose with the advice of your accountant. The second period will generally be 12 months ending on a date that then becomes your usual 'year-end'. Your accounting period need not coincide with the normal tax year starting 5 April. There may be some advantages, if your business is seasonal, to fix your tax year accordingly. If, for example, your highest earnings occur in the last quarter of the year you might wish to start your year on 1 October so that you have plenty of scope for tax planning in the following nine months.

SELF-ASSESSMENT

Self-employed people and business partners are required to retain their records for about six years and the Inland Revenue's advice is that such records should include:

▌ All sources of income including private income as well as business earnings

▌ Payments for which you will claim tax relief

▌ Bank and building society interest and dividend vouchers

▌ Business expenses plus sales invoices and receipts.

Your accountant will be able to advise you on the requirements for self-assessment. The Inland Revenue's self-assessment Internet pages are a comprehensive and authoritative source of information and assistance on all aspects of self-assessment.

TAXATION UNDER A CURRENT YEAR BASIS

New businesses are taxed from the start on a current year basis. For companies paying tax under the current year basis the payment dates are 31 January and 31 July. Tax is paid as two estimated payments (based on the previous year's tax liability) and a final balancing payment (or repayment) to bring the estimated payments in line with the actual due. Thus two payments are likely to be due on 31 January – a final balancing payment and an estimated payment. As such, a large amount can be due at once. It is therefore important to ensure that adequate funds are available to meet this liability as fines and interest are charged for late payments.

CORPORATION TAX

A company's profits each year are liable to corporation tax. The company's profit is defined as its sales income less its business expenses. The 2004 rates of corporation tax are as follows: nil on the first £10,000 of profits; 0–19 per cent on profits between £10,001 and £50,000; 19 per cent on profits between £50,001 and £300,000; 19–30 per cent on profits between £300,000 and £1.5 million.

For a new business the start-up rules will, depending on the accounting year end, result in some profits being taxed twice. Relief for this will only be given when the business ceases or the year end is changed. A 31 March or 5 April year end avoids this problem and should make your tax affairs easier to follow.

The profits taxed in your first year (the tax year during which you commence business) are those arising from the date the business started to the following 5 April. For the second year the profits arising in the 12 months to the accounting year end which falls in the second tax year are taxed. If there is not a full 12 months before the year end then the first 12 months of trade will be taxed. For the third year you are taxed in the normal way – on the profits for the accounting year ending in that tax year.

TRADING EXPENSES PRIOR TO SETTING UP

If you are a sole trader or partnership setting up a business, you are entitled to count as part of your trading expenses any relevant money you spent up to three years before you actually started trading. As a budding consultant you may have spent money on getting your brochure and stationery printed before launching your new career. These costs can be offset against the income that you eventually generate when you start trading. If you do make an income tax loss you can carry it forward against the future income from your consultancy. If you have other income in the same year as you make the loss, you can set the loss off immediately against that income. Furthermore, if you make no income tax loss in the first four years of trading it can be carried back and set off against your other income in the three years prior to the loss. But you cannot set a capital loss against income.

INCOME TAX PROFIT

The two most important rules for determining the profits of your business for income tax purposes are:

▌ Capital expenditure is not an allowable deduction.

▌ The only expenses which are deductible are those incurred wholly and exclusively for the purpose of the business.

These rules are discussed more fully below.

Capital expenditure

For income tax purposes a distinction is drawn between capital expenditure and revenue expenditure. In very broad terms, expenditure is capital when the value is not used up in the course of the year, and it is revenue when it recurs regularly year by year. Examples of capital expenditure are the cost of purchasing equipment, such as computers/word processors or fax machines, or the cost of purchasing a vehicle.

Although the cost of business equipment and vehicles cannot be claimed as a deduction in arriving at the amount of the profits, there are special allowances for the expenditure. These reduce the income on which tax is chargeable. You should seek advice from your accountant on the scope for claiming capital allowances.

When a car is used for both business and private purposes, a suitable division of capital allowances and running expenses has to be made. The tax inspector will need information about business and total mileage so that the division can be properly calculated. Journeys to and from a regular place of work are regarded as being for private, not business purposes.

Business expenditure

The rules for business expenditure are as follows:

(a) Only business expenses can be deducted from income to calculate taxable profits.

(b) Private or domestic expenses on items such as food, clothing and medical treatment are not allowable.

(c) Other expenses that are not allowable include premiums on personal insurance policies, income tax, any salary paid to yourself and your own National Insurance contributions, and the costs of business entertaining.

(d) Expenses which are allowable include accountancy fees, advertising, bad debts, employee's salaries, hire purchase charges, incidental costs of raising loan finance, insurance premiums for the business, National Insurance contributions by employers, pension contributions for employers and employees, repairs, travelling expenses incurred wholly in connection with the business, including vehicle costs attributable to the business.

(e) Heating, lighting, rates and telephone costs are allowable in full if they are wholly incurred in running the business. If, however, you are working from home, you will only be able to claim a proportion of the expenses.

(f) If you employ your wife or husband in the business the salary paid is an allowable expense, provided that the amount is appropriate and reasonable. PAYE has to be deducted and National Insurance contributions paid in these circumstances.

VAT

You must register with Customs and Excise for VAT if the value of your output is likely to exceed certain limits. In the March 2004 Budget statement, the threshold for registration was set at £58,000. You should start charging your clients VAT and keep VAT records as soon as you know you are required to register. The 'VAT Pack' supplied by your local VAT office contains all the information you need about registration and administrative procedures. The following is a summary of the main points to be considered.

To register or not to register?

You have no choice but to register if your outputs are or are likely to be above the limit. You can register if you are below the limit but it does require a lot of paperwork and Customs and Excise have the right to refuse to register you. Some consultants register as a matter of course to demonstrate to their clients that they are in business in a reasonably big way. If in doubt, seek your accountant's advice.

The VAT system

Once registered, you must charge VAT at the current rate of 17.5 per cent on all the fees and expenses for your consultancy services. Your invoices must show your VAT registration number and full details of your charges, separating your fees from the VAT charge. There are simplified requirements for invoices under £100, but you are not likely to be invoicing amounts below £100 frequently, if at all, so these arrangements will not concern you.

You will, of course, be paying VAT yourself on business purchases and you must keep all the invoices you receive on which VAT has been charged and list them in a day book. At the end of each VAT accounting period (usually quarterly) you must complete a VAT return of all your outputs showing their total value and the amount of VAT charged. Against this, you can set off the total value of your inputs (VAT on your purchases). If the value of your outputs (the amount of VAT paid to you) exceeds the value of your inputs (the VAT you have paid on your business purchases), you must pay the balance to Customs and Excise. If, on the other hand, you have paid more VAT on legitimate business expenses than you have received, you can claim the difference from Customs and Excise.

You must keep adequate VAT records, including the relevant documents. They will have to be produced if a VAT officer carries out an inspection. Customs and Excise require you to keep all business records for a period of at least six years.

Recent changes aimed at helping small businesses include the annual accounting and cash accounting schemes. The annual accounting scheme aims to reduce the paperwork involved with VAT returns by requiring only one annual return. However, estimated payments must be paid more frequently. The scheme is available for new businesses with an annual turnover subject to VAT that is not expected to exceed £150,000, and for existing businesses with a turnover subject to VAT that is between £150,000 and £660,000. Businesses using the scheme may continue to use it until their annual taxable turnover reaches £825,000.

The cash accounting scheme allows the VAT return to be based on the amount of VAT received and paid rather than the amounts invoiced. This scheme is designed to help cash flow. The cash accounting scheme is unlikely to benefit a business that expects a repayment of VAT or is usually paid as soon as a sale is made.

If in any doubt about VAT consult your accountant or your local VAT office.

NATIONAL INSURANCE CONTRIBUTIONS

Self-employed individuals, including active partners, normally have to pay Class 2 contributions, and Class 4 contributions on profits between certain limits, defined in the guidance available from the Inland Revenue. Class 2 contributions are paid at a flat rate of £2.05 per week. Class 4 contributions are paid at a rate of 8 per cent of annual profit between £4,745 and £31,720 and 1 per cent on profits above £31,720.

EMPLOYEES

If you have any employees you will have to operate the PAYE system and also pay National Insurance contributions. For up-to-date information consult Inland Revenue guidance on PAYE for employers.

10

Insurance

Proper risk management means planning for potential problems and attempting to insure against them. You should be familiar with the numerous types of insurance available, the method of obtaining the insurance, the best way to reduce premiums, and the pitfalls to avoid.

OBTAINING INSURANCE

Insurance companies market their services chiefly through the methods discussed below.

Agencies

These are the small, individualized operations that place home, car, or other common types of insurance with several insurance companies to which they are contracted. In some cases, small agencies, to earn their commission, are under an obligation to place a certain volume of insurance with each company they deal with. Therefore, it is possible that you might be sold policies offered by companies that may not suit your needs and may not necessarily be priced competitively.

Insurance brokers

Insurance brokers claim to have complete independence from any insurance company and more flexibility than the common agencies. In comparison with agencies in general, brokers from the larger companies are more knowledgeable about and flexible in the types of coverage and policies they offer, and they specialize in certain areas. Also, a broker should have no vested interest in placing insurance with any particular company and will therefore attempt to get you the best price and the best coverage to meet your needs. You should make specific enquiries to satisfy yourself.

As in all matters of obtaining professional advice or assistance, you should have a minimum of three competitive quotes and an opportunity to evaluate the relative strengths and weaknesses of each. If the brokers are using the same insurance base for the best coverage and premiums, then all three brokers should recommend to you, in theory, the same insurance companies for the different forms of coverage you are requesting.

PLANNING YOUR INSURANCE PORTFOLIO

It is important to consider all criteria to determine the best type of insurance for you and your business. Your major goal should be adequate coverage, avoiding both over- and under-insurance. This is done by periodically reviewing risk and keeping your agent informed of any changes in your business that could potentially affect your coverage.

The following principles will help in planning an insurance portfolio:

(a) Identify the risk to which your business is exposed.

(b) Cover your largest risk first.

(c) Determine the magnitude of loss the business can bear without financial difficulty, and use your premium expenditure where the protection need is greatest.

(d) Decide what kind of protection will work best for each risk:

– Absorbing risks
– Minimizing risks
– Insuring against risks with commercial insurance

(e) Insure the correct risk.

(f) Use every means possible to reduce costs of insurance:

– Negotiate for lower premiums if loss experience is low
– Use excesses where applicable
– Shop around for comparable rates and analyse insurance terms and provisions offered by different insurance companies.

(g) Risk exposure changes, so a periodic review will save you from insuring matters that are no longer exposed to the same degree of risk. Conversely, you may need to increase limits of liability. Review can help avoid overlaps and gaps in coverage, and thereby keep your risk and premiums lower.

(h) If you are pleased with a particular broker who can handle your various forms of insurance, it is preferable to be selective and have just one firm. An advantage of the larger broker firms is that they have a pool of insurance professionals, expert in various areas, whom you can call on as resource people.

(i) Attempt to keep your losses down in every way. Although your business may have adequate coverage, losses could be uninsurable, exempt from coverage, or have a large deductible. Problems with insurance coverage could seriously affect the survival of your business.

TYPES OF BUSINESS AND PERSONAL INSURANCE

The types of insurance you might need will vary widely according to the type of consulting practice you have. The following overview of insurance policies is provided to make you aware of what exists and of what might be appropriate in your situation. As mentioned earlier, these types of insurance are not necessarily recommended. Only you can make that decision after an objective assessment of your needs following comparative research in a competitive insurance market.

General liability

Most liability insurance policies encompass losses such as:

(a) Money you must legally pay because of bodily injury or damage to the property of others.

(b) All emergency, medical, and surgical expenses incurred from the accident.

(c) Expenses for investigation, your defence, settlements, and a trial.

A general liability policy covers negligence causing injury to clients, employees, and the general public. The policy is normally written up as a comprehensive liability policy.

Products or completed operations liability

This policy offers protection against a lawsuit by a customer or client who used your product or service and, as a result, sustained bodily injury or property damage from it.

Errors and omissions liability

This coverage protects you and other professionals against litigation arising from losses incurred by your clients as a result of an error or omission in your advice to them.

Malpractice liability

This insurance protects you from claims arising from any losses incurred by your clients as a result of negligence or failure on your part to exercise an acceptable degree of professional skill.

Motor insurance

This coverage includes other people's property, other cars, persons in other vehicles, and persons in the insured vehicle.

If you are using your car for business purposes, exclusively or occasionally, it is important that you have your premium cover business use. It is possible that your current motor vehicle insurance policy has a premium based on personal use only. Problems could occur if there were an accident and it was discovered that your car was indeed used for business purposes.

Fire and theft liability

You probably already have fire and theft insurance if you are working out of your home as a consultant. If you are working in an office or an apartment, it is important to make sure that you have satisfactory coverage.

Business interruption insurance

The indirect loss from a fire or theft can be greater than the loss itself. If your premises or files are destroyed, you can lose revenue. Certain expenses must still be met. Such a situation could put a severe strain on working capital and seriously affect the survival of the business.

Business interruption insurance is designed to cover the period between the time of the loss and the return to normal operating conditions. The insurance policy could also include the costs of temporarily renting other premises.

Overhead expense insurance

Consultants whose business income would cease if they were temporarily disabled by illness or accident may take out insurance to cover the cost to them of their fixed business expenses or overhead which have to be met even when they are unable to earn income.

Personal disability insurance

You could possibly be disabled for a short or long period of time. This insurance pays you a certain monthly amount if you are permanently disabled, or a portion of that amount if you are partially disabled but capable of generating some income.

Key person insurance

The death of a key person could seriously affect the earning power of your consulting practice. For example, if you have an associate, partner, or sub-consultant who is critical to a particularly large project or your business as a whole, life insurance should be considered.

If the key person dies, the loss may result in a decrease of confidence by your existing or potential clients, leading to a loss of future contracts, competitive position, and revenue, and the expense of finding and/or training a replacement. The amount and type of insurance will depend on many factors, as designing an evaluation formula for a key person is difficult.

Proceeds of the key person policy are not subject to income tax generally, but premiums are not a deductible business expense.

Shareholders' or partners' insurance

If it is your intention to have a partner in your consulting practice or a shareholder in your company, you may wish to consider shareholder or partnership insurance. Normally this type of insurance is part of a buy–sell agreement that allows for a deceased shareholder's or partner's interest to be purchased by the surviving partners or shareholders of the corporation.

In the absence of a buy–sell agreement funded by life insurance, the death of a partner could cause the immediate dissolution of the partnership in law. Unless there is an express agreement to the contrary, the surviving partner's duty is to liquidate the business, collect all outstanding accounts, pay off all debts, and account as trustee to the personal representative of the deceased partner for the value of the deceased's interest in the business.

In the case of a company, the deceased shareholder's interest would be considered an asset and would go to the beneficiary outlined in the will, if a will existed. Naturally, the introduction of a new shareholder who owns an interest in the company, especially a majority interest, could have a very traumatic effect on the shareholders and the company's continued operation.

In summary, the procedure is that each partner shareholder applies for a life insurance policy on the life of the other. The applicant is the beneficiary and pays the premiums on his or her partner's life insurance policy. When a partner dies, the funds from the insurance are received tax-free by the beneficiary (the partner). These funds are then used to purchase the deceased partner's share of the business. The surviving partner retains control of the business, and the heirs of the deceased get cash for their interest.

Business loan insurance

In many cases your lender will be able to provide you with insurance coverage for the outstanding amount of your loan and will then incorporate the premium payments into the loan. In the event of your death, the outstanding balance of the loan is paid off.

Term life insurance

This type of insurance insures a person for a specific period of time and then terminates. The most common period is five years. If the insured dies within the term of the policy, the insurance company pays the full face amount to the heirs. The costs of premiums are based on life expectancy for the person's age during the five-year period. Term life does not have a cash or loan value.

Because term life insurance can be written for various time periods, and because of inexpensive premiums, it is valuable to the business person. Such term policies are often used to provide collateral security for loans to the firm or for personal obligations.

It is wise to have term insurance in the amount of at least your personal and business financial obligations for which you have a direct or contingent liability. This area is frequently overlooked.

Medical insurance

It is important to take out sufficient medical coverage for your needs. If you are doing any consulting assignments outside the country, you should have extended coverage that pays for medical bills that may be incurred by injury or illness.

Group insurance

You may be eligible for group insurance rates if you have four or more employees. The policies of insurance companies vary, but medical and dental plans are available for small groups.

Workers' compensation insurance

If you have a number of employees, you should make certain that you are covered by workers' compensation insurance if you are eligible. With this coverage, the insurer pays all costs that the employer is required to pay for any injury to the employee. The insurer also covers the employees for all benefits and compensations required by the appropriate laws.

If you have failed to pay your employer's portion of the insurance coverage, or have failed to meet your responsibilities adequately to your employees in terms of safety, it is possible that you as the employer could be held liable for any injury to the employee as determined by the common law as well as under workers' compensation laws. Employee coverage and the extent of the employer's liability vary considerably.

11

Professional liability

Consultants have the same degree of potential for lawsuits against them as do other professionals such as doctors, accountants, and solicitors. Claims could be made that the consultant was responsible for a wrongful act or omission or professional misjudgement. Professional liability claims may be brought by the client or by third parties such as investors, creditors, or lenders.

If the consultant is doing business as a sole trader or partnership, liability extends to the consultant personally. It may also extend to the consultant's estate after death. Liability can also extend to persons who were the consultant's partners long after the error or omission occurred. The statute of limitations in many jurisdictions will not begin until the claimant discovers or should have discovered, or knows or has reason to know of your alleged mistake.

As a consultant, you must weigh the degree of risk involved in your specific area of practice. Obtain expert legal and insurance advice about the proper methods of protecting yourself.

CONTRACT AND TORT LIABILITY

It is not uncommon for a consultant to be sued for both breach of contract and tort liability.

Contract liability

A claim made against a consultant by a client could be based on the allegation that the consultant failed to perform the services described in the contract in a reasonable and prudent manner. This liability involves only those who are parties to the contract, and it applies whether there is a verbal, implied, or written contract.

For the client to succeed in the claim against the consultant, all of the following elements must be proven:

▌ There was a valid contract between the client and the consultant. This contract, as mentioned earlier, could be verbal or written.

▌ The consultant materially failed to perform his or her obligations under the contract.

▌ The client suffered damages as a result of the consultant's breach of obligation.

In actions brought under a breach of contract, it is irrelevant in most jurisdictions whether the consultant's breach was innocent, negligent, or wilful. The client need only prove that a material breach of contract occurred and that damages resulted. There are, of course, numerous defences a consultant can raise depending on the particular circumstances. The amount of damages assessed against the consultant would be an attempt to restore the client to the position held if the contract had not been breached.

A consultant can be sued for breach of contract, for example, if the precise duties and responsibilities or services required under the contract were not met exactly as detailed in the contract. This is a good reason to make certain that a contract is written, not verbal. In a verbal contract it is difficult to establish exactly what the terms of the agreement were.

Another example is a consultant who signed a fixed price contract for a service to be provided by a certain date. If the consultant miscalculated the fixed price and abandoned the project before it was completed, he or she could be sued. This is not uncommon among new consultants unfamiliar with the skill required in preparing a fixed price proposal.

Tort liability

Tort liability is a violation of civil law rather than a breach of contract. Liability in tort is incurred toward the public at large. Any third party who has suffered through the direct or indirect actions of the consultant can make a claim against the consultant even if no contract existed with the consultant and the claimant had never met the consultant. For example, if a consultant submits a report with recommendations to a client and the client follows the recommendations, expends a large sum of money, and subsequently loses the money, the client's creditors, investors and lenders could attempt to sue the consultant for losses suffered (damages) due to negligent advice of the consultant. It would have to be shown that the consultant knew or reasonably should have known that others would be seeing the report with recommendations, and they would be relying on that report before investing or lending money.

For the claimant to succeed in a claim against the consultant, all the following elements must be proven:

▌ The consultant owed the claimant a duty of care.

▌ The duty or standard of care was breached.

▌ Measurable damages resulted from the breach.

▌ There was a direct connection between the breach of duty and the damages that occurred.

In a suit based on tort, evidence introduced into court must establish that the consultant departed from the local custom and standard of practice. If a consultant is found to be negligent, the court will attempt to compensate the claimant for the damages incurred.

REASONS FOR CLAIMS

Counterclaims

In many instances when a consultant sues a client to collect overdue fees, the client will counterclaim. The client may have a valid reason for not paying the fee, but very often the countersuit is intended to create delay and act as a leverage mechanism for settlement.

Conflict of interest

A consultant could be liable if it can be shown that the consultant had a vested interest in the outcome of the recommendations. For example, a client requests a computer consultant to review existing hardware and make recommendations for replacement. The consultant recommends replacement equipment. At some later point the client learns that the consultant received a large payment from the distributor of the product line for recommending a very large order. The client could sue the consultant for the undisclosed profit; if it could be shown that the recommended hardware system was not the appropriate system in the circumstances, there could be additional liability on the consultant's part.

Conflicting interest of clients

A consultant could be working for two clients who are in competition with each other. If it can be shown that confidential information was disclosed or the benefits of assistance to one client were at the expense of the other client, then possible liability of the consultant could be present.

Delegation of part of contract to employee or sub-consultant

The primary consultant is responsible for the work of employees or agents under the primary consultant's control. If the client maintains that the consulting work was not done, or not done properly by the employee or sub-consultant, legal action can be taken against the primary consultant.

Third party damages

If a third party such as a creditor, investor, or lender suffers damages as a consequence of the recommendations of the consultant to a second party, a third party can sue in tort.

Unclear expectations by client

It is possible that a client has unclear or unrealistic expectations of the work to be performed by the consultant and of the benefit to the client. This lack of clarity can be a basis for dispute if the performance was not perceived to be related to expectations.

HOW TO AVOID PROFESSIONAL LIABILITY AND PREVENT LOSSES

Although the possibility of being exposed to legal liability cannot be totally prevented, it can be substantially minimized by implementing effective administrative systems and procedures.

Many professionals concentrate on the technical aspects of their profession. Good management is equally important. Consideration must be given to proper staffing, training, invoicing and debt collection, and office procedures such as keeping diaries, checklists, and properly written records of every aspect and phase of the consulting business. As well, it is important to stay within the limits of your training, experience, and expertise. Do not take on work that is beyond your capability. Some good management techniques that can help keep you out of trouble are discussed here.

Client control

Clients who habitually try to avoid paying fees by claiming that errors have been made, or clients who frequently resort to litigation can be costly for your business. Make sure that you have control over the areas for which you are responsible. In other words, do not assume responsibility for matters that your clients control.

You should implement a prescreening process to select clients. Ways of prescreening are covered in chapter 16.

Cost estimates

Avoid giving firm cost estimates for activities arising from your services if possible. Depending on the type of consulting practice you have, you could be locked into a situation where a fixed cost has been given and the project suffers an overrun. Architects and engineers especially should avoid giving firm quotations.

Carefully drafted contracts

It is most important that a consultant operate with written contracts with clients. The contracts should be drafted carefully and based on competent legal advice. Contract ambiguities and misunderstandings are a major source of professional liability claims. Letters of understanding or contracts should be sent out to the client for acknowledgment and signature and returned by the client.

Free opinions

Be careful not to provide free opinions without knowing all the facts. You could be put in a position of being liable, even though you were not officially retained and had not received any fees. If it can be shown that someone relied on your advice and subsequently suffered because of your advice, you could be held liable.

Law

Make sure you understand the law pertaining to your specific work. For example, if you are performing consulting assignments overseas, different laws may apply that could create problems for you.

Sub-consultants

Sub-consultants should be carefully selected. Check to see that they carry adequate professional liability insurance. Make sure your insurance covers any work performed by a sub-consultant.

Records, systems, and procedures

Effective systems for your files, records, invoicing, and office procedures are essential for any business. See chapter 8 for specific ideas on how to keep your records straight.

Continuing education

It is important that the consultant develop more expertise and training on an ongoing basis through various professional development and continuing education courses. This shows a professional attitude and desire for knowledge and current information.

Quality control

The consultant should set up some system for monitoring the activities and performance of employees or sub-consultants. If a system is in place, this will show that you have developed a high standard of care in the operation of your business.

Communication

Effective communication helps eliminate many client problems. This topic is covered in chapter 16.

PROFESSIONAL INDEMNITY INSURANCE

The procedures outlined in the previous section, if implemented, should substantially reduce the risk of professional liability. However, professional indemnity insurance is necessary since the risk cannot be completely removed. Professional liability coverage should indemnify the consultant for losses and costs involved in the defence of claims.

Many clients insist upon their consultants holding professional indemnity cover, and will often define a required minimum level of cover, say £1 million. Professional institutions too generally require their members to hold and maintain this form of insurance.

The liability insurance coverage is limited to claims 'arising out of the performance of professional services' including errors, omissions, and negligent acts. If you provide a service outside the specified designation for your speciality, the insurance coverage could be voided.

There are many provisions in the policy that should be thoroughly explained, and if you are not completely satisfied, alternative coverage should be considered. The seven most important factors that have to be reviewed in selecting or analysing a professional liability insurance coverage are:

(a) Declarations

(b) Exclusions

(c) Insuring agreements

(d) Definitions

(e) Limits of liability

(f) Excess

(g) Policy conditions.

Your premiums can be reduced in a variety of ways, some of which are discussed here.

Excess

The greater the excess, the less expensive the policy premium should be. Check to see if the policy deductible applies to each separate claim or just once a year.

Comparing prices

There is competition in the marketplace for professional liability coverage. Make certain that the reduced premium presented to you does not reflect less attractive provisions in the policy that you may not understand. Again, you should obtain professional advice from independent sources to satisfy yourself as to the nature of the coverage that you are getting. It is a prudent investment to have a lawyer who specializes in insurance law review the proposed insurance terms and conditions.

Changing the type of coverage

Claims made policies are generally less costly than occurrence policies. The reason is because the claims made policy covers just claims made during the policy term. The risk, therefore, to the insurance company is reduced compared to occurrence coverage.

In occurrence coverage, the insurance company's risk is considerable as a claim can be made against the insurance company many years after the negligence occurred and after your policy expired. The cost of settling a claim long after the event could be much higher than a settlement today. It is this risk and uncertainty on the part of the insurance company that is passed on to you in the form of higher premiums for occurrence coverage.

PRACTISING WITHOUT INSURANCE

Some consultants choose to conduct their business without any professional liability insurance. If the degree of exposure and risk is very low, this might be a viable alternative. If the consultant has very few personal assets and is effectively judgement proof, then personal bankruptcy may be an alternative in the most extreme circumstances if a claim is made.

Incorporating a company and conducting the consulting practice through the company should add some protection in a lawsuit if the company lacks any assets. The danger of operating a consulting business that has a risk element but no professional indemnity insurance is the uncertainty if problems occur. A client or third party could sue the consultant personally as well as the company and, until the trial, you would not know what the outcome would be. In the meantime, you would have to incur the costs and pressure of the process. In other words, conducting a business through a company is not an automatic guarantee of personal protection. The other uncertainty is the nature and amount of damages that your advice caused your client or third parties. It may be very difficult to project at the time you are conducting a consulting assignment what the financial damages could be if your advice is in error.

If you do intend to practise without professional indemnity insurance, it is most important that you receive expert legal advice to maximize your protection in advance.

12

Credit, invoicing, and debt collection

Many consultants starting out in business are more interested in performing their skilled service than in developing a clear credit, invoicing, and debt collection policy. In many cases a consultant has had no previous business experience and does not realize the pitfalls that can occur.

A system rigidly followed is essential to your survival. It does not take many bad debts to completely eliminate the profit of the business for the whole year. In more serious cases, you could go out of business if a substantial debt owing by a client is not paid.

A number of common mistakes are made by inexperienced consultants. First, the consultant, wanting to build a clientele and reputation as quickly as possible, takes on many clients, performs the service, and incurs expenses, but allows the client to defer payment. Second, the new consultant may be too busy or too inexperienced to monitor payment carefully. Third, unpaid bills are not followed up quickly with appropriate steps to collect funds. The effect of this sloppy approach can be disastrous.

This chapter outlines the pitfalls to be aware of and the procedures to adopt when reviewing your debt collection policy. If you develop the correct system for your needs, it will enhance your cash flow and profit and minimize stress, client problems, and bad debts.

DISADVANTAGES OF EXTENDING CREDIT

When you extend credit, the understanding is that the client intends to pay, is capable of paying, and that nothing will occur to prevent the client from paying. You assume that most clients are honest and acting with goodwill and in good faith. Many of these assumptions may not be accurate.

There are a number of potential disadvantages to extending credit.

Extending credit may take a great deal of your time, and the administrative paperwork – checking references, monitoring and following up on slow paying clients – may be tedious.

The expense of credit checking and collection could be more than you wish or are able to pay. Expenses could consist of credit reporting agency fees and memberships, collection costs, legal fees, and time lost that you could otherwise spend generating revenue.

You will need to increase your working capital requirements to keep your business in operation because receivables from your clients may or may not be paid when you expect or need them. You will be paying interest on additional working capital that you may have to borrow to offset your decreased working capital.

ASSESSING THE CLIENT

It is important to be very careful about extending credit. Apply the following general guidelines to your business:

(a) Develop a clear credit policy for your business after consultation with your accountant and solicitor. Experienced professional advice is essential before you extend credit.

(b) Develop a credit application information sheet that has all the necessary information for your files.

(c) Consider joining a credit bureau as well as a credit reporting agency such as Dun and Bradstreet. Check into the past debt payment profile of your potential client in advance.

(d) Check references from your client if appropriate. Ask about the client's length of time in business.

(e) Ask the client if consultants have been used before and, if so, what method of payment was negotiated.

(f) Consider carefully the amount of credit being extended. The greater the amount of money unpaid, the greater the risk for you.

(g) If the work you do is highly specialized and you have very little competition, you have a lot of leverage in the nature of credit that you would be extending.

(h) If the client is a large institution or government, ask about the customary length of time for accounts rendered to be paid. Specify in your contract the exact terms of payment; government payments in particular can be delayed by bureaucracy for two or three months or longer.

(i) If the client requests deferred fees, you run the risk of default or other problems. Sometimes clients request a deferment of fees or payment because it is a large project, the client is suffering cash flow difficulties, or other considerations. If you are faced with a decision about deferral of fees, you should consider charging interest on the total amount, charging higher fees, requesting a sizeable retainer fee before you start the project, or obtaining collateral to protect yourself if your total fees are substantial.

(j) Consider the future benefit of a relationship with the prospective client. If there is a possibility of future contracts or contacts with other prospective clients, you may wish to weigh the benefits against the risks.

AVOIDING CLIENT MISUNDERSTANDINGS ON FEES

Communication is vital to minimize client misunderstandings about fees. Many consultants feel uncomfortable discussing money matters during the first interview with the client. Or sometimes consultants become so involved in the client's problem that the fee is not discussed. It is important that the amount of money you expect is understood and agreed upon by the client before you commence work.

Three ways to eliminate misunderstanding on the issue of services performed for fees are through communication, written contract, and invoice.

Communication

Communication is a critical element to a satisfactory client relationship. It is important that the subject of fees is discussed openly at the time of the initial interview and resolved so that the client feels satisfied with the final bargain. Ask potential clients if they have hired consultants in the past; if they have, find out the nature of the contract relationship that existed.

The interview should be followed by a letter of confirmation outlining the essence of the discussion about fees, among other matters. Progress reports should be sent to the client from time to time if the circumstances warrant it; copies of correspondence concerning the client should be sent to the client. If appropriate, try to involve the client with the project in some way so he or she feels a bond with you and sees and appreciates the work you are doing on an ongoing basis. This should minimize the risk of a client disputing your fees for services.

Written contract

A written contract must be signed before work is commenced. The contract can take various forms as outlined later in chapter 18. Basically, a letter of agreement or formal contract explains the nature of fees involved and the method of payment whether it is payment upon receipt, net ten days, or net 30 days.

Be very wary about financing a client; if at all possible, have payment upon receipt of deliverables. This should assist your cash flow and minimize risk of late payments. The contract should also state the interest that will be added to the outstanding debt if it is not paid within the terms of the contract. The contract should spell out in detail the exact services that you will be performing for the fee.

In certain circumstances a stop work clause could be inserted in the agreement to the effect that if payment is not made within the terms of the contract, at the option of the consultant all work will stop.

Finally, the contract must be signed by the client's decision-maker in authority. It is preferable that this individual be the same person with whom you negotiated the contract.

Invoice

To minimize misunderstanding on invoiced amounts, it is advisable to provide a detailed breakdown of the charges for services and expenses for the particular phase of the contract. If appropriate, reference should be made on the invoice to the contract agreement on fee structure and method of payment.

Late payment legislation

UK legislation (The Late Payment of Commercial Debts (Interest) Act 1998) allows a business, whatever its size, to claim interest on an account outstanding for more than 30 days, provided that the customer has been made aware of its payment terms before work is contracted. The rate of interest is calculated as the Bank of England base rate at the end of the last day of the 30-day term plus 8 per cent.

MINIMIZING RISK OF BAD DEBTS

There are several effective techniques to minimize the risk of bad debts. As discussed previously, most consultants cannot afford to have one or two nonpaying clients without seriously affecting the viability of the business. The following general guidelines may not all be appropriate in a given client situation. Your judgement in each individual situation must dictate the appropriate approach.

Advance retainer

A client can be asked to pay a retainer or deposit of 10 per cent to 25 per cent or more of the total contract amount prior to the work being performed. This can be justified on the basis that you are very busy and if you are going to schedule in a commitment to that client, it is your policy to require an advance commitment retainer.

This is an effective technique for a potentially high-risk client who has a reputation for nonpayment or late payment, or who constantly argues about bills. This approach can also be considered when dealing with a new client who has not used consultants before.

Prepaid disbursements

Depending on the length of the job and the type of client, you may wish to request prepaid disbursements if they are going to be sizeable. You do not want to fund the client for out-of-pocket expenses at the risk of your own cash flow. You also do not want to run the risk of a nonpayment or dispute of the overall account. As mentioned earlier, it is one thing to lose your time; it is another thing to be out-of-pocket.

Progress payments

It is common for consultants to request funds by means of invoicing at specific points in the project. The stages at which progress payments are to be paid would be outlined in the contract.

Regular invoicing

Statements can be sent out on a weekly or monthly basis, depending on the circumstances. It is important to outline in the contract, if appropriate, your policy on the timing of invoices. That way the client will not be taken by surprise. This also provides you with the advantage of knowing at an early stage in the consulting project if the client is going to dispute your fees, and at this point you can either resolve the problem or discontinue your services. It can be very risky to allow substantial work to be performed, or to wait until the end of the project, before rendering an account.

Invoicing on time

Generally a client's appreciation for the value of your services diminishes over time. This is a common problem. It is important, therefore, to send your invoice while the client can see the benefit of the service you have provided. Present your final invoice at the completion of the project.

Accelerated invoicing

If you sense that the client may have problems paying the bill, or if other factors cause you concern, accelerate your normal invoicing pattern. You want to receive payment on your account before difficulties can appear.

The risk of rendering an account that states 'net 30 days' is that the client is not legally overdue in payment to you until after 30 days. If you become aware of client financial problems, it is difficult to commence legal action before the 30-day period has expired.

Withholding vital information

If you have documents, records, reports, and other material related to the client and the project, you may feel it appropriate, if circumstances warrant, to withhold returning all the necessary material to the client until your account has been paid or other appropriate arrangements made.

Holding up completion of important stage of project

If client problems occur, you may wish to stop providing your services and resources at a critical stage until the matter has been resolved to your satisfaction.

Personal guarantee of principals of a client company

Depending on the project and client, you may want to have the principals in a client company sign a formal contract as personal guarantors. Another variation is to have the contract in the name of the client company and its principals as co-covenanters of the contract.

Monitor payment trends of clients

Record and monitor the payment patterns of clients so you can watch for trends that may place your fees at risk.

Follow-up of late payments

If you see an invoice is more than a week or ten days overdue, begin the various steps of your collection system immediately.

Involving client in assignment

As mentioned previously, try to involve the client in some fashion during each step of the project. By making your client aware of your services, benefits, time, and skill, you should minimize problems that could occur because of an unbonded or remote relationship.

INVOICING FOR SERVICES

Invoicing requires a system that is carefully designed and effective. It is important to have a third party review your invoicing procedures before you open your business. Examine your invoicing procedures on an ongoing basis, especially during the first year, to make sure they are effective. This also gives you an opportunity to review your fee arrangements to make sure you are bringing in the appropriate cash flow for the time you are spending. As mentioned previously, it is important to monitor each client's file to see general trends in your client payment patterns.

Proper records must be maintained that detail the time and expenses incurred so that the invoice can be prepared at the appropriate time. You should have an established procedure for regular invoicing so outstanding accounts are rendered on a regular basis, thereby minimizing collection disputes or bad debts.

When rendering an invoice, make sure you send the account either directly to the appropriate person who has the authority to pay your account, or deliver the invoice personally to the client. Your style, the client, and the circumstances will determine the most appropriate approach.

You may choose to send a general invoice to your client outlining briefly the services performed, the number of hours, the expenses, and the total fee. A note on the invoice might say, 'detailed particulars are available upon request.' See Sample 13 for a detailed invoice.

Your invoice should be rendered on your consulting firm's stationery showing your name, address, and telephone number. Always use stationery, not a blank piece of paper with your name typed on it. Prepare three copies of the invoice. Send the original and a copy to your client and keep a copy for your files.

The wording on your invoice should include the following, assuming that you are registered for VAT:

(a) The tax point (date of invoice)

(b) The name and address of the person invoiced

(c) An outline of the services performed

(d) The consultants or other resource personnel who performed the services

(e) The date services were performed, and the total hours worked

(f) Total charges for services

SAMPLE 13

DETAILED INVOICE
(PRINT ON FIRM'S STATIONERY)

Smith Jones & Associates

To: Mary Roberts
Chief Executive
ABC Ltd
10 London Road
Anytown, Anywhere

Tax Point:
File reference:
Invoice number:
Terms: Net cash

Re: Computing System Analysis

PROJECT CONSULTANT: John Smith

Professional services: £

July 15	Attendance at South Branch site to review operations (4 hours)	300.00
July 17	Meeting with Ms Roberts to discuss findings (3 hours)	225.00
July 19	Attendance at South Branch site to analyse operations (5 hours)	375.00
July 22	Preparation of report and recommendations (8 hours)	600.00
July 26	Meeting with Ms Roberts to review recommendations (3 hours)	225.00
July 30	Prepare final report of recommendations (7 hours)	525.00

Total professional services (30 hours @ £75 per hour)   £2250.00

Expenses:
Car mileage (343 miles @ 35p per mile)   120.05
Sub total   2370.05
VAT @ 17.5% on above   414.76

Total   £ 2784.81

VAT registration number...

(g) Expenses necessarily incurred (itemized)

(h) Total of fees and direct expenses payable by client

WHY CLIENTS PAY LATE

If you have established appropriate precautionary measures and a credit and invoicing policy, you should have very few overdue accounts. However, overdue accounts will occur in any practice, and understanding your options should minimize your problems in this area.

There are several common reasons why a client might be late in paying for consulting services. The client could be indifferent to your deadlines. Some clients have a sloppy attitude about paying accounts due and are accustomed to being pressured or reminded frequently before they finally meet their obligations.

Institutional or government payment procedures sometimes involve a two- or three-month wait for accounts to be paid. This type of information is easily available by asking the right questions before you begin. Your account may be lost in the maze and require personal attention.

A client may deliberately delay payment in order to save money at your expense. You save the client interest on working capital if he or she can use your money for free. This is why you should have an interest factor for overdue accounts built into your initial contract as well as showing on the statement. If the overdue interest is high enough, that should act as an incentive for the client to pay on time. If this is in the contract, the client cannot argue that there was no agreement on overdue interest. Rendering a statement with the interest factor noted on it is not in itself evidence of an agreement between the parties on the amount of interest on overdue accounts.

A client may prefer to give priority to other creditors, where pressure to pay is greater.

The client may not have the money. This does not necessarily mean that the client is going out of business, but is cash poor at the moment. The technique to handle this problem is discussed in the next section.

COLLECTING LATE PAYMENTS
WITHOUT LEGAL ACTION

Because of the expense, time wasted, stress, and uncertainty of legal action, it is preferable to collect as much as you can from clients yourself. Some steps that you may wish to consider are:

(a) Send out a reminder invoice with a courteous comment that the invoice is 'overdue and that perhaps it was an oversight or the cheque is already in the post.'

(b) The alternative to the above is to telephone the accounts payable department or the client directly to ask when the payment can be expected. Courteously ask if there was possibly a misunderstanding, or if they need further information or clarification on any matter. Make sure that you note in the client file the date and time, the person you spoke to at the client's office, a summary of the conversation, and when payment can be expected.

(c) If you have not received payment within a week of the preceding step, send a letter stating that the account is in arrears and that it is to be paid on the terms of the contract. The alternative is to again telephone the client and ask about the reason for the delay.

(d) Another technique is to ask when the cheque will be ready. Say that you will be around to pick up the cheque or will arrange for a courier service to pick it up as soon as they telephone your office to advise that it is ready.

(e) If the client has still not paid, stopping work on the project is another option.

(f) If the client refuses to pay, legal steps may be required immediately depending on the size of the invoice, the importance of the client, the reasons for nonpayment, and the cost of legal action. Alternatively, you may decide to compromise with a client and settle for a reduced payment.

(g) If the client is unable to pay because of cash flow problems or other financial difficulties, you have to assess your options. If the client is not disputing the invoice and wishes to have credit, there are basically three options:

   (i) Instalment payment plan: the client would agree on definite dates for payment and would send you the amounts owing upon receipt of statements from you.
   (ii) Post-dated cheques: you would receive post-dated cheques from the client for the agreed period and amount.
   (iii) Promissory note: the client would sign a promissory note agreeing to the total amount of the debt and the date on which the debt would be paid. The note should be signed by the principals if the client is a company. Interest on the full amount of the debt should be built into the promissory note. It is negotiable whether or not interest is added onto the other two payment plans.

LEGAL STEPS IF ACCOUNT REMAINS UNPAID

If it is apparent that the client has no intention of paying you, is objecting to your invoice, or is unable to pay you, then legal action must be considered. It is critical that legal action be commenced as quickly as possible after it becomes apparent that you will not be paid by other arrangements. At this stage you are not interested in keeping the client for present or potential future business. You just want to salvage the best of a bad situation. There are basically three legal options available.

Collection agency

You may wish to assign the debt to a collection agency for which you will be charged a large proportion of the amount collected. This is better than writing the account off as a total loss. Different agencies have different styles of collection, and one agency may achieve better results with your bad debts than another. If your client pays you directly during the period of the contract with the collection agency, you are obliged to pay the commission to the collection agency. Collection agencies are listed in the *Yellow Pages*.

Small Claims court

The Small Claims court is a relatively quick, informal, and inexpensive method of taking your client to court. If you are successful and obtain a judgement against your client, that does not necessarily mean you are going to collect on the judgement. There are additional steps you will have to take, such as filing a judgement against the title of any properties owned by your client. Your client could turn out to be judgement proof.

Solicitors

Solicitors can be very effective in the collection of debts if you act promptly and select a lawyer who is experienced in the law and tactics of collecting. Solicitors generally invoice on an hourly basis, and the more time expended on attempting to collect a debt, the more money it will cost you without any assurance that you will be successful at trial. If you are successful and do obtain a judgement, your client could be bankrupt or judgement proof in terms of assets. As mentioned previously, the litigation process can be very protracted, uncertain, stressful, and expensive.

BAD DEBTS AND TAXES

Keep an accurate record of any bad debt accounts and the procedures you went through to attempt to collect. Generally you will be allowed to deduct bad debts from your other income, but this is a matter that should be discussed with your accountant as the laws and circumstances can vary.

13

Fees and estimates

SETTING FEES

The fees you are able to set – your fee structure – will be governed by the marketplace. There are two markets:

■ General market rates – the fees that different parts of the public and private sectors are prepared to pay for different types of consultancy services.

■ Individual market rates – the fees that can be charged by or for the individual consultant depending on his or her field of expertise, experience, qualifications and reputation.

General market rates

By whatever means possible you must get a 'feel' for market rates. Ask people you know who engage consultants, ask other consultants. Find out, if you can, what the big firms are charging in different sectors. You may discover that rates vary from sector to sector. Public sector organizations attempt to get away with lower fees and often succeed. The rates for international assignments may be different from those in the UK – greater or less depending on where they are.

Your market rate survey will show a wide range of rates. In 2003 large firms were charging out consultants at anything up to £1,500 a day and their managers and partners at a rate of up to £2,000 a day or perhaps more.

Sole practitioners and small firms generally charge out at a lower rate – the range in 2003 for established and professional consultants was typically between £500 and £1,000 a day. There are, however, amateurs, moon-lighters, part-timers and desperate redundant executives who try to undercut the market with fees of as little as £150 a day. And there are some exceptional people involved in strategic work who can charge more than £1,000 a day.

All these rates are subject to variation according to sector and location. Fee rates in London and the prosperous parts of the UK are often higher than elsewhere.

Individual market rates

The rates charged by sole practitioners mentioned above do, of course, vary with the marketability of the individual consultant. Those new to consultancy might find it difficult to charge more than £350 a day, unless they have had exceptionally relevant experience in their jobs prior to taking up consultancy, or enjoy a well-established reputation.

WHAT RATE SHOULD YOU CHARGE?

If you are a moonlighter or someone making a bit on the side you might be happy to charge as little as £150 a day. But if you are trying to make a reasonably good living out of consultancy you must aim higher than that. Remember that many people really believe that they get what they pay for. Your credibility as a consultant may well be related to the value you place on your services.

If you are a sole practitioner clients will normally expect you to charge lower fees than a large firm would for consultants with broadly equiva-lent experience and capabilities. Such clients will say that you don't have to carry the overheads of a large firm, although this could be a fallacious argument – there is such a thing as economies of scale. Perhaps more rea-sonably, they will claim that a large firm has back-up resources and access to databanks that you lack. The counter-argument that the quality of an assignment depends on the quality of the consultant and that you are providing a high-quality personal service does not always convince clients. It may well be the case that the sole practitioner can do as good a job, if not a better one, than a consultant from a large firm, but you may have to accept, reluctantly but gracefully, that you will be expected to charge less.

Clearly, although fees are largely market driven, you have still to charge at a rate which, based on assumptions about the proportion of your time you will be able to charge out (your utilization rate), will pro-vide you with the return on your investment time, energy and expertise and the standard of living that you want.

It will help you to make decisions on fees if you draw up a break-even chart as illustrated in Sample 14.

This indicates the revenues and break-even points you will achieve for different levels of fees and utilization rates. In this example it is assumed that the consultant:

(a) is a sole practitioner working from home using the minimum of secretarial help and able to keep nonrecoverable expenses down to £15,000 a year;

(b) needs to draw at least £30,000 a year from the practice to live on (a + b is the break-even point of £45,000);

(c) has 220 days of chargeable time available; this is calculated by deducting from the total of 260 working days in the year, 25 days' personal holiday, 8 public holidays, and 7 days for illness and conferences: 40 in all.

Varying fees

You should consider adopting a range of fee rates. The minimum rate could be fixed by break-even point analysis and an estimate of your market value in sectors where market rates for consultancy are low. The maximum rate could also be fixed by reference to the top market rate for your skills. You might, for example, wish to adopt a standard rate of £500 a day and be prepared to flex it between £350 and £750 depending on your assessment of the market, the client and your worth in a particular situation. You would have to be careful to be consistent in your charging practices with the same clients in a sector where information about fees might be exchanged.

Consultants sometimes charge less for long assignments where the work is guaranteed. This could be beneficial as long as the reduced fee rate is above your break-even point. Clients may ask for 'continuity discounts'. If this is a possibility, it is best to discuss terms in advance before committing yourself in a proposal. You want to avoid haggling afterwards.

Increasing fees

From time to time you will want to raise your fees. This could be based on your regular monthly, quarterly or other reviews of your cash flow statements, profit and loss statements or projected needs. Your utilization rate is also a factor.

If you are considering increasing fees, it is tactically a good idea to do it at a fixed time every year, such as 1 January. You should also attempt to notify your clients at least three months in advance, in writing, of your intention to increase your fees. Include a brief explanation about the reasons, such as an increase in costs, if appropriate. Invite the client to contact

SAMPLE 14

BREAK–EVEN CHART

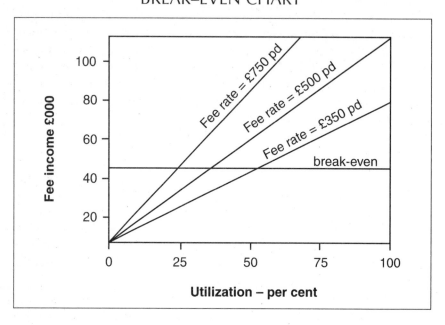

you if there are any questions. It is important, for obvious reasons, to keep the increase competitive.

Daily or hourly rate?

It is quite common to quote a daily rate, although there may be situations where you are giving intermittent services or advice or regularly working long hours where an hourly rate is more appropriate. If you assume a seven-hour working day, excluding luncheon, your hourly rate is one-seventh of your daily rate. You might want to round this up to take account of lack of continuity. When quoting fee rates it is sometimes useful to quote a daily rate, say £500, and indicate that part days will be charged pro rata, assuming a seven-hour day.

A daily rate suggests that if you are working full time for a client you charge no more if you work longer than your normal hours. You will be expected to work client hours and, indeed, should do so if the client is within easy reach of your base. In fact, you might find yourself working late with the client's executives. You should take this into account when setting your daily rate and decide to charge accordingly. Even when you are visiting clients for a day's work away from your base you will still be expected to travel mainly in your own time and get to the office or factory not much later than their normal starting time.

Travelling time

It is not customary to charge for travelling time for local journeys and if you are charging a daily rate it is generally assumed that this allows for travelling time and no more will be charged. If, however, the assignment involves visiting a number of sites in one day, it would be perfectly proper to charge for travelling time between visits. If there are special circumstances which you believe justify additional charges for travelling time it is essential to set these out in your terms and conditions or clear them in advance with the client as part of the contract.

Expenses

Your contract should state that expenses necessarily incurred during the assignment will be charged at cost. These can include travelling, overnight accommodation, subsistence, long distance telephone calls, printing, duplicating, computing, the preparation of manuals and training materials, and large-scale typing. You would not normally be expected to charge for local calls or small-scale typing (letters, memoranda, and brief reports).

You can reasonably charge for at least three-star hotels, first-class rail travel and club-class travel on overseas flights, but it might be advisable to clear the latter in advance with your clients and some might not be prepared to refund more than standard or economy-class fares. But they cannot object if you are incurring expenses at the level they would expect to allow for their equivalent executives. Charge mileage according to the AA scale for your car.

Clients may request an estimate of your expenses in advance. If possible, avoid giving too firm an estimate. Circumstances might arise in which extra expenses are necessarily incurred and you want to be able to recover them. Clients may ask you for evidence that the expenses have been incurred so you should keep a record of them and save your receipts.

ESTIMATING

One of the most critical but also the most tricky job a consultant has to do is to estimate the time required to complete the assignment, leading to the preparation of the total cost estimate. You do not necessarily have to provide your clients with a total cost and there are obvious dangers in working on a fixed-cost basis. Your time estimate may have been too modest or you may run into unforeseen snags that cause an overrun. In these circumstances, if you cannot get your client to agree to pay more, you either have to put in an excessive amount of unpaid extra work or allow the overrun to prejudice other assignments and limit your marketing activities.

Some contracts, such as the standard one issued by the Institute of Management Consultants, insert a clause to the effect that, although the estimate was prepared in good faith, it *was* only an estimate and is therefore subject to revision should unforeseeable circumstances arise. Such a clause might be helpful, but some clients will still argue that the contract was a fixed price one and that the consultant must live with it.

Preparing estimates

Time estimates should be prepared analytically; that is, the time taken for each activity in each stage of the assignment should be calculated, and the parts added up to produce the total time. For example, in a job evaluation assignment, you might need to prepare job descriptions for each benchmark job. Experience tells you that it takes about half a day per job (one hour for the interview, one and a half hours to prepare the draft and one hour to clear the draft with the job holder and his or her manager). If you have 20 benchmark jobs, you will take 10 days in all. The other components of the assignment could be estimated on similar lines. A complete estimate for the job would look like the example shown in Sample 15.

An estimate produced in this form provides a good base for monitoring the progress of the assignment. You should regularly compare actuals with budget so that you can take action as necessary to catch up with lost time.

It is advisable to add 10 per cent or so to your first estimate for contingencies, more if you are on unfamiliar ground. In the above example your estimate could be 25 days. If your fee rate is £500 a day the total estimated cost of the assignment would be £12,500 plus VAT plus expenses necessarily incurred in the course of the assignment.

Variations to estimates

Analytical estimating along the lines described is the best technique, but there will always be plenty of scope for variation. One of the factors you may need to take into account is how much clients will do for themselves. In a job evaluation assignment, for example, much of the work required to prepare job descriptions could be carried out by the client's staff under the consultant's supervision. The time estimates for this activity could then easily be halved.

There is often a range between the minimum time needed to do a basic job and the optimum time required for a 'Rolls-Royce' job. Judgement is required when deciding where to pitch your estimate. And in making pricing judgements you will have to take account of the competition (you are likely to be pitching for the job alongside three or four competitors)

SAMPLE 15
TIME ESTIMATE

Stage	Activity	Time – consultant days
1	Collect basic data	2
2	Prepare, issue and collect questionnaires	1
3	Prepare benchmark job descriptions	10
4	Carry out preliminary ranking exercise for benchmark jobs	1
5	Use analytical scheme to evaluate and grade benchmark jobs	1
6	Supervise preparation of nonbenchmark job descriptions	2
7	Slot nonbenchmark jobs into grade structure	1
8	Analyse salary survey data	1
9	Prepare salary structure	2
10	Devise salary administration procedures	2
		23

and the price sensitivity of your client. It is obviously dangerous to pitch too low, even if you are desperate to get the job. Low bids will only lead you into trouble later on and clients may not be impressed by what they could perceive to be a cheap and nasty approach.

One way to avoid frightening clients too much with the cost of your proposal is to provide an estimate of the fees for the basic job and then some optional extras. You can indicate in the proposal as strongly as possible the desirability of these extras but explain that a decision on incorporating them would best be made during the course of the assignment when what is needed will become clearer. This approach could impress your client, who would appreciate the fact that you are realistic enough to know that as a consultant you do not know all the answers from the outset and that some may only emerge after deeper analysis has taken place. The danger of this tactic is that the client might gladly accept the basic proposal and reject the extras, in which case you will have sacrificed an opportunity to get the extra work.

NEGOTIATING

Avoid negotiating fees if you possibly can, but clients will sometimes respond to your proposal with the request that you reduce its cost. You should not contemplate replying with an offer to reduce your fee rates. Neither should you reduce your time estimate. To do so would be to imply that you had over-estimated in the first place. The only approach open to you in these circumstances is to reduce the scale of your contribution to the project. This could take the form of cutting out or postponing any parts of the proposal that are not essential to achieving its fundamental objectives. Alternatively, you could suggest that a higher proportion of the work involved should be carried out by the client's staff under your supervision. Obviously, you should not contemplate either of these tactics if you believe it would prejudice the success of the assignment. Your professional integrity must be given priority, even if it means losing the job. You should never allow yourself to be put into the position of haggling over fees. In any case, clients who haggle are not the sort of clients you want to have. However, there are clients who quite genuinely can only work within a budget which has been imposed upon them, and there will be circumstances when, without sacrificing your professional standards, you can tailor your proposal to their needs.

INCREASING PROFITS WITHOUT INCREASING FEES

There are many ways in which you can increase your profits apart from raising fees. Naturally, clients are not always going to appreciate your reasons for increasing your fees, so through careful tactics other effective methods could be used to increase your profits. Some methods you may wish to consider are as follows:

▌ Keep your overall fixed overheads down. Consider the ways of saving costs on space, telephone and personnel.

▌ Use company cars, space and supplies wherever possible.

▌ Obtain the client's agreement to supply necessary support services such as secretarial and clerical, post rooms, postage, delivery services and other support services and personnel. This will keep your administration costs down.

▌ Obtain approval to charge authorized purchases relating to the project to the client.

▌ Keep an accurate record of all out-of-pocket expenses incurred pertaining to the client's project, document them and invoice for them properly.

▌ Arrange with the client to pay you in advance for any necessary travel expenses you anticipate.

▌ If you are consulting on an hourly basis, attempt to arrange to be at your client's office or project for a full day if possible, rather than a portion of the day.

▌ Bear in mind that transportation costs and time of travel are not always accurately reflected in the adjustments with the client.

▌ Determine a minimum fee requirement. The time and costs of a proposal, and the administrative work required by a project, will dictate a minimum fee and profit before you make a proposal.

▌ Avoid giving away free consulting. There are techniques to avoid giving away your time, which is worth money. This will increase your effective utilization rate and therefore increase profits. Various ways of avoiding free consulting are covered in chapter 17.

▌ Increase your rates for work requested outside regular business hours. A premium fee should be charged for work performed at weekends, during evenings or for part of a day. This suggestion also applies when clients ask that their project be given priority over other projects.

▌ Consider obtaining advance payment on account for projected initial or total disbursements if they are considerable. The deposit can be collecting interest for your benefit. As discussed previously, you should consider negotiating in advance for a sizeable deposit if your services are in demand and you are expending time for the client at the expense of other client work you could do.

▌ Review your credit policy regularly. If you extend credit, make sure your receivables are promptly collected; otherwise you will be paying more interest to the bank on your overdraft or loan.

▌ Try to minimize bad debts by adopting the various procedures suggested in chapter 12, with modifications for your own situation and after your solicitor's advice. Eliminating bad debts is a very effective way of increasing your profits.

▌ Consider negotiating a bonus with a client for meeting contract needs. For example, if you complete a project for less than the amount allocated in the budget, you could negotiate a percentage of the saving. If your client has deadline schedules, you could agree to give the project priority, which would involve considerable overtime and other disruptions for you, and negotiate a bonus for the number of days you are ahead of the deadline.

14

Determining market opportunities

Before determining market opportunities and identifying clients with accuracy and success, various matters have to be considered.

You have to be very certain in your own mind of your area or areas of specialization. It is impossible to target your market without this basic information. Review the exercises in chapter 2 to determine your specific skills, talents, and attributes, and attempt to visualize the market that is suited to your abilities. It is important to avoid the tendency to be too restrictive in your view of the market for your services. Look for a wide spectrum of opportunities to apply your services in vertical and horizontal markets and in both the public and private sector. Identify common themes and processes. Know why there is a demand for consulting services so you can aim your marketing at those concerns when targeting prospective clients.

Thorough research is required to educate yourself and stimulate your mind on the wide range of possibilities. Read selected newspapers, magazines, and trade journals on a regular basis, and look for consulting opportunities created by political, economic, and social changes affecting your area of expertise and interest.

The next chapter discusses marketing techniques in more detail. This chapter is intended to provide a brief overview of the private and public sectors and the possibility of market opportunities.

PRIVATE SECTOR

There are numerous opportunities in the private sector. By being aware of the issues and problems and solutions in your service area, it will be easier for you to identify and think of opportunities every time you are exposed to information through personal communication, television, radio, newspapers, magazines, trade journals, or books. The habit of training yourself to be aware of marketing opportunities at all times is essential.

It is important to understand the motivating factors that will cause a potential client to want your services. You might be very aware of the needs of your service within your specialized area, but a client who does not recognize that your service is needed will not be receptive to your offer of assistance.

There are many reasons that motivate a client to retain a consultant, but three of the basic reasons are to obtain information, to save time, and to save money. If you can visualize the ways you can save a client time and money, and provide the most current and accurate information in the client's area of interest and need, market opportunities in the private sector will be considerable.

Individuals

Individuals buy the services of consultants in a wide variety of fields. A walk through the *Yellow Pages* should provide a good example. Advice on how to save money or how to make money is fairly common. In this instance, the target market is anyone in the higher earning bracket, including executives and professionals. Some examples of consultants in this area are tax consultants, financial consultants, investment consultants, and property consultants. Other consulting areas include interior design and fashion.

Small businesses

Small businesses provide an excellent client base for a new consultant. The failure rate of small businesses is very high. The small business owner/operator's lack of knowledge in important areas of small business management is often a factor. If your skills include small business management and making or saving money in a small business, you can find a market. There are numerous books available on small business management that will provide ideas for you. Some are listed in appendix 3: Further reading.

Various techniques can be used to attract small business clients. You can offer a fee based on percentage of savings or profits that occur as a result of your advice. Naturally, you would have to have a measurable basis for showing the positive benefits that your advice has created. A percentage fee is a good marketing device. It shows confidence in yourself and it is a difficult offer to refuse as your payment is based on performance.

Small businesses also need to raise funds, either through the venture capital market, commercial banks, or government grants and loans. Most small businesses go through growing pains. Wherever business growth occurs, problems occur, and wherever problems occur, a need exists for solutions.

Medium-sized businesses

There is a high demand for consultants in medium-sized businesses. Companies often hire experts as required instead of hiring staff. Hiring staff involves the related costs of training, benefit packages, and long-term commitments for possibly short-term needs. Businesses are vulnerable to economic changes, and their survival is based on keeping overheads low and making a profit. Any areas of need you can identify to increase efficiency and productivity and sales and to decrease overhead and losses will create a demand for your services.

Medium-sized businesses, as well, are constantly going through various stages of growth with all the predictable problems involved.

The advantage of dealing with a medium-sized business is that projects tend to be more lucrative. There is also a greater chance of repeat business. Another advantage is that the decision-makers are generally more sophisticated than small business owners, better able to see the need for a consultant more readily, more accustomed to dealing with consultants, and able to respond more quickly on proposals.

Large companies

It is more difficult to obtain contracts from larger companies. Many large companies prefer dealing with large consulting firms or well-known consultants with considerable experience and contacts.

Because of the money available in larger businesses, consulting opportunities do exist, particularly in the area of temporary technical assistance. It is common for consultants to large companies to have developed their experience and confidence with smaller and medium-sized companies before marketing to the larger companies.

PUBLIC SECTOR

Government is a major user of consulting services. Marketing opportunities are available in various forms in the public sector. You can submit a solicited or unsolicited proposal and attempt to get the contract directly. You can indirectly benefit from government by subcontracting with other companies who have been awarded the main contract. An additional way of making money through government is as a grants consultant assisting organizations or businesses to obtain grants or subsidies.

If you are considering government as a source of business, you should be aware of the various ways of obtaining contacts or information to assist you. You should also understand the way the government approval system operates.

Making contacts and obtaining information

There are various steps you can take to obtain the necessary information and make the necessary contacts to assist you in your government dealings.

(a) Read government advertisements and publications pertaining to your areas of interest.

(b) Place your name on mailing lists. There are numerous government departments and you can request that your name be placed on each list to receive all relevant information, including proposed procurements and contracts awarded relating to your field.

(c) Attempt to have your name placed on the government sourcing list as a consultant in various specialized areas. There are various computerized sourcing lists throughout the departments of government; make sure that your name is on all the ones that relate to your areas of interest.

(d) Contact government contract officers. Most government contracts are awarded at the department or agency level where the specific needs are best known and money has been allocated. The phone book has listings for various branches of government. The public library has updated lists of all the key government departments, individuals, their titles, and phone numbers. Once you have obtained the correct department, ask to speak to the contract officer who can provide you with further background.

(e) Visit government departments and agencies. After you have submitted your CV to various government departments, you may wish to introduce yourself to the person in charge of approving contracts. This may or may not be appropriate or possible, depending on your geographic location and government policy. Maintaining contact with the key person who could award a contract shows your interest in keeping your name current. It also demonstrates initiative and confidence. On the other hand, it could cause irritation or you could discover you have a personality conflict. (In which case you may decide that you don't want to pursue contracts with this person.)

(f) Contact large consulting firms that are the recipients of government contracts and might require additional consulting assistance for those contracts.

(g) Contact other companies that have recently received a government contract. You can discover the names of these companies by consulting the EC Official Journal (Supplement S), which contains information on the contracts that have been awarded, who received the contract, and the amount and nature of the services to be performed. With this information, you can determine what subcontracting opportunities might be available in your specialized area and immediately contact the companies concerned.

(h) If you have friends or acquaintances who work in government, tell them you are looking for consulting assignments related to your specialization. You should also provide them with your CV and a brochure if possible. They might be in a position to inform you if they hear of an agency in need of your services. You might therefore hear of a need before the department has advertised for services or selected a consultant. You can then submit an unsolicited proposal.

(i) Make yourself known to your local Business Link office and download current information from the Business Link website.

Understanding the government approval system

The government approval system is very formal and bureaucratic in its operation. Most government contracts are awarded only after a call for proposals, whereas in the private sector, submitting an unsolicited proposal is the most common method of obtaining work. The general procedure for government approval is given below. The procedure is the same for any level of government (ie, local or national).

(a) A government department head or agency requiring consulting service assigns personnel to an internal search to see if the service can be performed in-house.

(b) If no civil service employee is available to perform the work, a request for proposal is advertised, proposals are received, and the consultant is eventually selected. It is quite common that consultants are 'preselected' before the closing date of the advertisement. This is because the consultant may already be on the source list and be known as best suited for the project. The advertisement is a required government formality.

(c) The department drafts a contract and submits it to the consultant for review and signature.

(d) The signed contract is reviewed and approved again by the legal or procurement unit.

(e) A contract is forwarded to the head of the division for approval.

(f) The contract and specifications are forwarded to the government purchaser for approval.

(g) The contract and fee schedule are forwarded to the government controller to verify that funds are available and have been set aside to honour the payment commitment.

(h) Notification of formal approval is sent to the consultant to begin the consulting services within the terms of the contract.

(i) Work begins and is completed.

(j) Payment is received at the end of the project or throughout the project, depending on the terms of the contract. Many departments are slow to pay because of the bureaucratic nature and requirements within the system for approval before payment. As this may cause cash flow difficulties for you, you should make arrangements for progress payments if at all possible. If necessary you can get a bank loan for your cash flow needs based on the strength of a public sector contract.

GRANT CONSULTING

A grants consultant attempts to obtain grants, loans, or subsidies for a client. Government and its various agencies award large sums of money to eligible applicants. The process followed by grants consultants is as follows:

(a) The consultant learns as much as possible about the sources of funding, the amount of funding, the procedures required, and the key contact people. The consultant contacts the funding unit and obtains information on the appropriate or desired detail and format for successful applications.

(b) The consultant determines the potential target market and the names of the firms and individuals who could be future contacts.

(c) A personal letter with brochures is sent to the key people, followed by a telephone call and meeting if possible.

(d) The consultant identifies the specific needs of the organization or company in the interview process. The interview process is similar to that described in chapter 16.

(e) The consultant advises the organization of the availability of funds and the consultant's expertise in obtaining them. Most organizations and businesses do not have people who realize that money is available or know how to effectively submit an application to obtain it. The consultant performs the analysis, collects all the necessary detail for documentation, and prepares the application for signature by an authorized representative of the organization or company.

(f) The consultant normally takes an administration fee that is a negoti-ated percentage of the amount awarded. The client therefore has an incentive to deal with the consultant, because the consultant's fee is based on performance only and paid from the funds received.

(g) The consultant could also be responsible for coordinating the imple-mentation of the programme on which the funding was based, if applicable.

(h) Once a grants consultant has succeeded with one group, marketing to all other organizations similar to that group can be effectively performed.

Government aided grants

The Business Support Directory maintained by Business Link has a guide to obtaining grants, which outlines the types of grant available, the basics of grant eligibility and applying for government support, as well as the pitfalls to avoid when applying for grants. The Directory also provides access to a database of grants and subsidies. The grants currently available in the UK include research and development grants, innovation grants and funding for organizations that aim to improve the quality of life for those in need and to help tackle social exclusion.

15

Marketing your consulting services

WHAT YOU NEED TO MARKET YOUR SERVICE

Marketing, the stimulus that creates an awareness of and demand for your services, is essential for success in the consulting business. This process involves a wide spectrum of activities, ultimately directed at convincing prospective clients that their needs can be met and their problems can be solved by your specific services. Selling is one part of the marketing programme that is intended to result in a consulting assignment by means of personal interaction begun at the initial interview and maintained during and after the assignment.

The dynamics of the marketing/selling stages have to be clearly understood and cultivated by the consultant. For example, when you are marketing yourself, you have to calculate the image that you want to project when you are packaging your product, that is, yourself and your services. You and your marketing efforts must project authority, confidence, friendliness, candour, expertise, competence, and leadership.

Many consultants fail, or maintain a marginal income, because of poor marketing. Consultants frequently do not appreciate the necessity of marketing, do not know how to market, do not like to market, do not want to market, or do not take the time to market.

This chapter will help you understand the various techniques required to build your image as an expert or authority, thereby creating a demand for your services. The next chapter covers some of the personal selling techniques involved in the first interview. Once your marketing plan has stimulated the interest, the next step is to close the contract.

MARKETING PLAN

A summary of the factors that go into your marketing plan follows:

(a) Define your skills and services. This is covered in chapter 2. You should have a clear idea now of the nature of services you will be offering potential clients. You may have decided on just one particular area of interest and specialization, or you may have decided on several areas that you will promote either to the same client or to different categories of clients.

(b) Target prospective clients. Identifying possible client consulting opportunities is the next step in the marketing plan. This was covered in the last chapter.

(c) Make potential clients and the general public aware of your services, and create a demand. The various techniques required for this step are covered in the next section.

(d) Respond to enquiries with direct client meetings. Naturally, once interest has been shown by a prospective client due to your effective marketing, your next step is to follow up on the lead quickly, personally see the client if that is possible, attempt to ascertain the client's precise needs, and determine how to remedy the problem.

(e) Prepare a proposal. This step follows the preceding one, confirms the client meeting, and outlines what you intend to do, how, for how much, and when. You can only write a convincing proposal after you have had an opportunity to ascertain the client's needs and the benefits that you can provide.

(f) Perform the project. This is the purpose of the whole marketing exercise – to end up with the client so you can provide your service, generate revenue, and make a profit.

(g) Follow-up is the final step in the marketing plan. If you did not obtain a contract after your previous attempts to market, you should maintain some follow-up procedure in case the client needs your services in the future. Possibly there were budget constraints the first time.

If you were able to obtain a contract and provide a service, you should have a follow-up routine in place to encourage repeat business with that client. Open communication with the client is important to ensure goodwill and possible referral business.

MARKETING TECHNIQUES

The following suggestions describe traditional as well as unusual ways of marketing consulting services. Many of the techniques cost little or nothing except for your time. Whether you use just a few of the techniques or all of them depends on your style, your priorities, the nature of your service, and your type of clientele.

Newspapers

Most consultants do not use newspapers as a source of advertising for their services. It is looked upon as unprofessional by many. Most clients select a consultant by reputation. But it depends on the nature of your consulting business. For example, if you specialize in small business cash flow problems, and if there are small businesses with problems in your area, you might put a tasteful, professional advertisement in the display ads in the business section or in the classified section to stimulate interest.

Advertising in trade or professional journals

The advantage of advertising in these publications is the very specialized market you reach – the readers could all be potential prospects. Therefore, the cost/benefit feature of this form of advertising can be low. You should attempt to get all the trade and professional journals related to your area of skill and services and familiarize yourself with the format and the nature of the journal ads.

Directories

There are many excellent reference guides listing technical, professional, and trade organizations and associations. Many of the organizations listed in the directories publish annual directories of their memberships.

Of the organizations that have directories, approximately half of them will include your name in their directory free of charge as a consultant in that area of interest. Most of the other organizations have paid advertising available, which could be of benefit if the directory is read by a prime segment of your market.

Brochures

Brochures are a very important part of marketing your practice. There are many ways to use a brochure.

(a) Leave the brochure with a prospective client after a face-to-face meeting.

(b) Post the brochure after a written or formal request for further information.

(c) Send the brochure in a direct mail campaign targeted to prospective clients.

(d) Distribute the brochure at a seminar or presentation you are giving.

(e) The day after a seminar or presentation, send the brochure out to those attending as a form of follow-up communication.

Keep in mind that your brochure is probably the first contact a prospective client has with you and the services you offer. The reaction to the brochure may be positive or negative, depending on its format, content, and quality. Following are some tips on preparing a brochure:

(a) As first impressions are critical, it is important that the layout, graphics, and paper be of top quality. You want to stimulate a desire in the recipient to retain you as a consultant, or at least to enquire further.

(b) The size and format of your brochure is a matter of choice. But it should not be too long. You don't want to bore your readers. If you can have an attractive cover and say all you need to say in four 8" x 5" pages, so much the better. Obtain advice from typesetters and graphic designers and printers before you finish your draft. Seek out comparative opinions and quotes until you are satisfied with the quality and cost offered. The design of the brochure should be consistent with your stationery and business cards.

(c) The phrasing of the text should reflect a confident, positive, dynamic yet professional tone. Have the spelling, grammar, syntax, and style of your text reviewed by someone with skills in that area.

(d) The text should be concise, clear, and brief. Text in bullet point form can be easily read. Refrain from using large or complicated words. Keep the words simple and direct. Focus on the benefits that a prospective client will receive from your services. Draft the text from the viewpoint of the client's needs.

(e) Provide information on the history of your business, the nature of your business, your clientele, and the type of services you perform. Explain why a particular service might be required. Explain or list the benefits that you can give to provide the service and meet the need or resolve the problem. Think of previous clients who benefited from your advice and assistance.

(f) List your academic and professional achievements and experiences.

(g) Do not list your associates unless you have a long-standing relationship or know that they will be staying with you for an extended time. Refer instead to the resource base of talent your firm offers. You may wish to itemize the skills that are provided by key associates.

(h) If appropriate, a number of testimonials from clients, or a list of important clients, could be included in the brochure.

(i) Many consultants prefer not to have their photograph in the brochure as a matter of personal choice and style. The reaction of a potential client to your brochure could be negative or positive based on your picture alone.

(j) Before you have the brochure printed, have a number of your friends, relatives, and business associates look at the draft copy of the brochure and obtain their candid feedback.

Direct mail

Direct mail can be a very effective means of making potential clients aware of and interested in your services. There are several advantages to direct mail: the cost is flexible, the sales message can be personalized to the needs of that particular target group, and with a word processing program, letters can be individually addressed to specific persons. An important cost/benefit aspect is the controlled circulation to a very select audience.

The first step is to develop and/or acquire a mailing list. The most cost-effective way may be to build up your own list of contacts and past and present clients. But it may pay you to extend your target audience by renting a list.

Mailing lists are often rented from list brokers for one-off use, and are 'seeded' by means of fictitious companies or individuals to ensure you do not use the list longer than the time contracted. For further information consult the *Direct Mail Directory* of *British Rate and Data* (*BRAD*).

The various directories of organizations related to your specialization may also rent or sell mailing lists. The advantage of this type of mailing list is that prospective clients may be members of the organization that publishes the directory. You would therefore be targeting your services to your specific trade or interest market.

There are a number of specialized direct mail advertising agencies listed in *BRAD*. For a fee, they will determine the best mix of mailing lists for your purpose, depending upon the amount of money you are prepared to budget. They can obtain the best rates for you and for an additional fee will prepare your mail shot, but this can be expensive.

Response rates can be very small – less than 1 per cent unless you have a very specific and well-presented proposition which is sent to a highly selective list. Many other factors will decide your response rate, such as the type of consulting service you provide, the economic climate at the time, the cyclical or seasonal demand for your type of service, and the techniques and format you use in the direct mail approach.

There are various stages involved in direct mailing, all of which are equally important to obtain the desired objective. The basic steps are as follows:

(a) Your first mailing should be within the regional area you can realistically service. It is also an opportunity to test market and analyze the effectiveness of your mailings without spending a large sum of money.

(b) Your mailing should consist of a personalized cover letter (printed on a word processor if available) addressed directly to the key decision-maker. Use quality letterhead stationery to create a professional impression. You might also enclose your business card. Enclose a copy of your brochure with your letter. Outline briefly the services you offer and the benefits that will be obtained by the prospective client. State that you will contact the client within ten calendar (or business) days to answer any questions and discuss the matter further at that time.

(c) Keep an accurate filing system of all prospective clients you intend to follow up on. List all pertinent information on the card so you can review it and familiarize yourself with it before you contact the client. Note the date you will contact the prospective client in your daily calendar.

(d) Follow-up with a telephone call ten days after you mail the letter. This will give the client a positive impression of your administration and professionalism. Follow the telephone call with a visit to the prospective client if circumstances allow. The next chapter outlines other procedures and techniques to follow before, during, and after the first meeting with the prospective client.

(e) If the response to your mailing is poor, thoroughly review all your techniques and format. This includes the direct mail target group, cover letter, brochure, telephone techniques, and meetings.

(f) Constantly revise, refine, and upgrade your mailing list with new prospects.

(g) Send out mailings on a quarterly basis (or more often) as your finances, marketing plan, and other circumstances dictate. This will remind people of your services and expertise, and the repetition ultimately does have an effect. When sending out repetitive mailings, consider enclosing a newsletter, which you could easily prepare, and copies of any articles or other papers pertaining to the industry that is your target base. You may want to have a tear-off coupon in the newsletter that readers can send back if they want to be put on your newsletter mailing list. This way you should be able to track the response. Over time, a large portion of qualified prospects should respond to regular and consistent promotional efforts.

Contact network

You need to develop a contact network to develop future prospects and a mailing list. It is a very effective way to acquire clients by referral. Studies have shown that a high percentage of a consultant's clientele come from referrals through a contact network or from satisfied clients. A contact network is a collection of relatives, associates, and acquaintances who will give you an introduction to, or pave the way to your acceptance by an organization or individual who needs your services.

You already have a network, and you can cultivate many more contacts. A partial list includes past and present clients, employees, professional colleagues, business associates, bankers, solicitors, accountants, friends, neighbours, and relatives. Also included are contacts you develop in associations and social, professional, trade, business, or other organizations. If you sit down and list everyone who comes to mind as a potential contact, the list will be longer than you think.

Developing the contact network is the most effective and inexpensive way of increasing your exposure and credibility. Continually update your network by adding leads and other contacts to your mailing list.

Membership in professional, trade, or business associations

Joining a group and then actively participating in meetings and other functions is an effective means of developing leads. Attempt to attend meetings regularly and get involved in discussions. Evaluate a group or association on the basis of potential consulting prospects who are active in the association. You want to look for members who are likely to give you consulting opportunities. Because of the time commitment involved to develop your reputation within an organization, you must be very selective in your membership. Limit your memberships to one or two. You may wish to consider civic or trade organizations or local Chambers of Commerce. Obtain a list of all the members of the organization and review the list thoroughly. Most lists provide the name, position and company, type of business or profession of the member, and address.

Donating your services

You may wish to donate some consulting time and commitment to a worthwhile nonprofit organization as a gesture of goodwill. Naturally, you have to be very cautious about the time involved relative to the potential benefit, but your services without charge can enhance your image and result directly or indirectly in referrals.

Attending public and professional meetings

Consider attending meetings covering a subject directly related to your field of expertise. You want to see and be seen. Plan to contribute your opinion, if appropriate, in a well-planned, concise, and intelligent fashion. Prospective clients could be attending the meeting. Attempt to identify and talk to people you believe are worthwhile contacts.

Lectures

Many organizations or associations need speakers for breakfast, luncheon, or dinner meetings, conferences, or conventions. Look in the *Yellow Pages* under 'Associations' to obtain appropriate names. Also, review directories of associations available at your local library.

When you contact the chairperson, offer your services for free and advise him or her that you have a number of prepared talks you believe would be of particular interest to the membership. Mention that your subject areas are topical and interesting, and your talk can be between 10 and 30 minutes long. This is the normal range of time required for a speaker. Ask about the mix of membership and the number of members who normally attend meetings. Attempt to get in advance a list of members to review so that you can direct your comments more accurately toward your group.

It is helpful to have ready two or three 10- to 20-minute presentations with supporting material. You will then be available at short notice for any presentation.

The object of the presentation is not to make money, but to obtain contacts and increase your credibility and exposure for future consulting opportunities. Those who attend the presentation will probably tell their friends or acquaintances about you if your presentation is interesting. Make sure you tell the audience that you are a consultant. During your presentation you can give a number of examples or anecdotes based on your experiences. This will reinforce your image as an expert. People will remember you better by the examples or stories that you relate.

You may also wish to consider participating in public speaking courses or workshops to enhance your communication ability. For more tips about presenting your ideas in front of an audience, check with your public library.

Teaching

There are many opportunities to offer your services as a part-time or occasional lecturer. You generally get paid for your time, but ideally the students who attend the course will be potential clients or will recommend you to friends or associates. Make sure that you teach adults only to maximize the potential benefit. You are primarily looking for credibility, exposure, and contacts. The preparation required to teach a course also keeps you current on your subject area.

Seminars and workshops

You may wish to consider offering your own seminar or workshop. You can offer the seminar for free or for a nominal charge. The people who attend are excellent potential clients. You should try to select a subject that allows you to provide a practical overview of important tips and ideas within your specialized area. You can promote your seminar through your direct mail list. Allow four to eight weeks lead time to ensure that people can schedule in your seminar.

Other items to consider are the length of the seminar; the location; the time, whether day or evening; when refreshments would be served, if any; and the number of people you can accommodate. Make sure your announcement states that space is limited and available by advance registration only. In your announcement you can request that registration be made by phone one week in advance of the seminar. This will give you some idea as to the response and assist you in the preparation of your material. (If your registration deadline is one week before the seminar and not enough people appear to be interested, you can try to negotiate a cancellation arrangement with the hotel facility by paying a portion of the room rent, or possibly nothing at all, if the hotel is able to rebook the facility.)

You may also wish to consider the free advertising possibilities in the local newspaper and other monthly or weekly publications. If you allow yourself enough lead time, you should be able to conduct the seminar at a modest cost. Depending on the number of people and the amount you are charging, you could break even on the seminar.

Make sure you distribute your brochures, newsletters, and any other appropriate material at the seminar. Develop a seminar evaluation form where participants can give their opinions of you and your seminar topic through rating scales and space for additional comments. Also include questions that will provide you with biographical information on the participants. Attach a coupon to the seminar evaluation form for participants to complete if they wish to be kept on your mailing list for newsletters. Also have a space on the form to ask what particular areas of interest or concern a participant might have. This should assist you in developing other seminars or improving the existing one.

When a person phones in to register prior to the seminar, and on the day of the seminar, make sure that you get the full company name, address, phone number, and name and position of the person attending. You will want this information for your mailing list.

Free media exposure

There are many ways to obtain free media exposure. Exposure provides you with credibility and develops public awareness of you as an expert or authority in one or more areas. If a seminar or presentation is offered, either through your own company or through some other organization, consider preparing a news release. Send it in advance to the appropriate radio, television, newspaper, or magazine contact person. Determine who the contact person is and call in advance so he or she will be expecting your letter or news release. This also gives you an opportunity to introduce yourself and to make sure that the approach you are adopting will obtain the desired free exposure.

Ask the contact person what format is preferred for the information required. Spell out in your letter, and in your conversation, why you feel the topic of the presentation is of interest to the readers, viewers, or listeners. The subject matter may be topical or controversial.

Radio and television talk shows

You might also appear in person on a radio or television talk show. The same approach applies as in free media announcements. Locate the appropriate contact person and sell him or her on the benefits to the listeners or viewers of your being interviewed on the programme. If possible, try to be on the programme a week before your seminar or presentation in order to stimulate attendance. If the talk programme is too distant from the seminar date, the listener may forget about it.

Letters to the editor

It is easy to get published in the 'letters to the editor' section of a magazine or newspaper. Write a letter that is topical and relevant and reflects a controversial or divergent opinion. Refer to an earlier article if you are reacting to something previously published. Mention in the letter that you are a professional consultant in the field and have expertise in the subject area.

Writing articles

Writing is an effective way of developing exposure, credibility, and contacts. Once you have developed the format, style, and discipline, you should be able to write three or more articles a year for various publications. All publications are looking for articles; many do not pay very much, if anything, for unsolicited articles – but they will publish your work.

To locate magazines that have your target audience, look in your local reference library at *Willings Press Guide*, *British Rate and Data* and the *Writers' and Artists' Yearbook*.

Write an article about your area of expertise that you believe would be of particular interest to the readership of the publication. Use examples and stories in your article. The subject matter could be new trends, the effect of pending legislation, technical information, or any other angle that will enhance your image as an expert.

Contact the publishers of your targeted magazines or journals and obtain free copies so you can review them and familiarize yourself with their style and length. If your article is accepted for publication, request a byline and a brief biographical comment at the end of the article. Say that you are a consultant in your area of expertise, and invite questions or comments about the article. (Not all publications will permit this.)

There are numerous books on writing style. Have your article reviewed by at least one, if not two, friends or relatives who will candidly comment. Submit a good quality 5" x 7" glossy photograph of yourself and a biography with the article. Submit the article to one trade or business magazine at a time. Keep a list of editors at several trade journals and business magazines whose readership constitutes your potential target base. If one does not publish your article, send it on to the next editor on your list. When it is published, obtain extra copies of the publication to distribute in your next direct mailing or presentation.

Additional benefits to writing articles are the contacts you can make and the credibility you can develop as you go through the research process. For example, you could select 20 or 30 people to interview for background information for the article. These people could include key potential clients. Have a script ready before you phone them, ask open-ended questions, listen carefully and note their answers. Ask follow-up questions to their responses. This should show that you are knowledgeable and an intelligent communicator. When you contact prospective clients to interview them over the telephone, introduce yourself as a consultant writing an article. You can ask their opinion on matters such as the effect of pending legislation, unique problems they encounter in their field of interest, and major opportunities or trends they perceive.

The telephone conversation can be followed by a letter thanking people for their cooperation and assistance. Depending on the responses to your questions, you may see that many consulting opportunities exist with the people contacted. They may have mentioned some of their problems. At a comfortable time in the future, you may wish to contact these sources and follow up with a personal letter and brochure. You might feel it appropriate to say you will contact them ten days later to ask whether you may be of service. Subtlety is essential.

Writing a book

Having a book published is another marketing technique to establish yourself as an expert in your field. There are a number of limitations though. You have to find a publisher for your book or publish it yourself, which can be quite expensive. Your book could be obsolete by the time it is published, as the lead time before publication can be lengthy. The time you would have to spend on the book might not be justified in terms of the cost/benefit due to loss of income or potential income. It could be far more beneficial to spend the time writing articles rather than a book. Regularly publishing articles also keeps your name in front of the public and reinforces your image as a specialist.

Have articles written about you

Every field of consulting has news value. By carefully cultivating relationships with editors and reporters, you could be looked on as an expert in your area. They might invite your opinion and quote you in an article on the topic. You could also have articles written about you if you can demonstrate a newsworthy feature, topical benefit, or uniqueness. Attempt to look for news angles that could have a direct or indirect effect on the public at large or your target group in particular. Look at economic, political, or legislative factors. Over time you could build up a reputation as an authority that will generate enquiries from prospective clients.

Announcement columns

Many professional, trade, or university graduate publications have sections devoted to announcements of interest about their members. Make a point of regularly updating information provided to these publications whenever you can find an excuse to justify it, if your style allows. If you give a presentation, expand the services that you provide, or announce new associates or distinctions, you can get your name inserted. If you are giving a seminar or workshop, give yourself enough lead time for an announcement to be inserted, if possible, in these publications. Many daily or weekly publications have a free announcement section available.

Newsletters

Newsletters are a very common way for consultants to promote themselves. They offer a subtle form of advertising that can give you credibility, as well as providing advice to readers. Most newsletters are distributed free since they are used as a marketing device. Once you establish a reputation and a large mailing list, economics and demand may justify charging a fee for a subscription.

The important features of a newsletter are effective use of colour and layout, a professional appearance, and well-written articles on interesting subjects. Most potential clients who will receive your newsletter are very busy; unless the newsletter captures their attention and is easily readable, it will not serve the purpose that you intend. The newsletter should have tips, news, ideas, and possibly a question and answer column. It should be two to six pages long, A4 or tabloid size, and published on a regular basis, such as monthly, bimonthly, quarterly, or semi-annually. The frequency of your publication will depend on your finances and time.

A newsletter is distributed in the same manner outlined earlier for brochures. When sending out brochures with covering letters in response to an enquiry, you should also include a recent copy of your newsletter. As in the case of direct mail marketing and brochures, you should address the newsletter to the key people in target organizations.

Website

As discussed in chapter 3, you may want to seriously consider the many marketing benefits of having your own website. Check out the *Yellow Pages* listing of consultants practising in the same field, by looking at consultant directories in your specified field, or generic consulting directories. All these directories should be available in your public library, from your professional association, or on the internet. Then research the websites of other consultants in your field, to determine how you can develop a better professional website that meets your needs and goals.

16

The client interview and client relations

Your efforts at marketing have now been successful. The prospective client is aware of your services and a meeting has been arranged, requested by you or the prospective client. The initial interview is a critical step before preparing a proposal and obtaining a contract. There are many important techniques that you will have to understand and adapt for your particular needs. This chapter covers the matters you should consider before, during, and after the client interview.

PURPOSE OF INTERVIEW

The purpose of the interview is primarily fact finding, followed by an analysis of the client needs and problem identification. After these steps, you will be able to prepare a proposal. The meeting, of course, has other purposes, such as assessing the prospective client's personality, ability to pay, and expectations. It also provides an opportunity for an interchange of ideas and mutual assessment.

BEFORE THE MEETING

If the client contacted you, you know a need exists and the client has some confidence in you. You should not have an interview over the telephone if at all possible. You want to have a face-to-face talk. Do not quote your rates over the phone, as they could be misinterpreted and the prospective client may not wish to continue to the next stage of the interview. If you are asked about your rates, attempt to defer an answer until the time of your meeting by stating that your rates vary depending on various factors such as estimated time involved, the type of work required, and whether the client is a profit or nonprofit organization. None of these factors can be ascertained accurately before an interview. In addition, there are different forms of fee structure that can be negotiated. This response should satisfy any enquiry.

The initial interview is normally free as a goodwill and marketing technique. Once a specific date and time have been set for the interview, confirm them in writing beforehand so no misunderstanding occurs. If the consultation is to be without charge, state that. Send your brochure with the letter. Your brochure should describe your background, past experiences, and nature of service and references, if you think that is appropriate.

There are specific steps to take to prepare for the interview.

Review the client's circumstances so you are familiar with them before the interview. Find out everything you can about the company, industry, and problems affecting the industry. Learn the client's jargon and way of doing business. You can obtain considerable information from business publications, annual reports, trade journals, newspapers, and other clients in similar industries.

Try to find out about the client's likes and dislikes, hobbies, memberships, sports, recreation, and travel. Look for clues of personal interest or accomplishment when you are in the client's office. If you can find common links, a basis for friendship can be quickly established.

Prepare specific questions to ask during the interview. Concentrate on client needs and problems. Some of the basic questions to ask include:

(a) Has the client used a consultant before? How long ago? What was the experience like? What was the purpose?

   If the client has not used a consultant before, you may need more time to convince the client, and there may be more problems to be aware of in working with him or her. If the client has used a consultant before and the relationship was a positive one, you should find out what particular aspects were considered favourable. If a previous consultant relationship was not satisfactory, you should find out the reasons for that from the viewpoint of the client.

(b) Has the project been attempted previously? If so, who attempted it and why was it abandoned? The assignment might be impractical or impossible to complete to the client's satisfaction.

(c) If a client had a past relationship with a consultant, what type of financial fee arrangement was negotiated? It is not necessary for you to know the actual sum, just the type of contract. You can then ask if that type of arrangement was satisfactory. That will provide you with guidelines on the type of fee arrangement to present in your proposal.

Naturally, you want to offer the kind of fee arrangement a client feels comfortable with. If you prefer a different type of fee arrangement, you will have to discuss the benefits of that with the client during the interview, if possible.

(d) What specific measurable results and benefits must be obtained for the client to feel satisfied? The nature of the change, what form it will take, and how long it will take must be clarified. It is essential that the expectations of the client be specific, measurable, attainable, and realistic.

(e) Has a time period for the proposed project been discussed, and is that possible within your time schedule and other commitments? Has the subject of the cost of the project in general terms been discussed? What was the client's tentative reaction? If the type of payment has been discussed, what are the terms?

(f) Has a discussion taken place about the client's responsibilities in matters such as availability of the client's personnel, equipment, and work area, etc.? Does the consultant report to a committee or to one person? Access to information resources is required in order to complete the project. Can that access be obtained and how? Has the client been effectively convinced of the consultant's role as an agent of change? Does the client demonstrate appreciation and respect for the consultant?

(g) Is travel involved?

(h) Do you feel confident that you are qualified and able to help the client?

(i) Do you feel comfortable that a clear understanding exists of the client's problem or need?

Try to understand and anticipate client fears or concerns in advance and deal with them. A client may have underlying biases about you as a consultant that could affect the interview and its outcome. By knowing in advance the fears that might exist, you can counter them directly during the interview and proposal stages. Studies have shown that the following anxieties often exist. They are listed generally in order of priority.

▮ A consultant may be incompetent.

▮ The client may be continually dependent upon the consultant once the first relationship begins.

▮ The consultant might assume or interfere with managerial control during the project.

▮ The consultant's fees are excessive relative to the services provided.

▮ The consultant may not be able to complete the project in time.

- ▌ The need for a consultant is an admission of failure on the part of management.

- ▌ The consultant might disclose confidential internal information.

- ▌ The consultant might have inaccurately analysed the needs and therefore will give an improper diagnosis.

- ▌ The consultant will lack impartiality.

Normally, a consultant will meet a client in the client's office. The client feels comfortable in familiar surroundings and is therefore more relaxed. The advantage to the consultant is he or she has the opportunity to view the client's offices and operations, and can leave diplomatically if the meeting is unproductive or continues too long.

Try not to have a meeting just before lunch, as the client could have a lunch commitment, be distracted by the time, or feel hungry.

Attempt to arrange an appointment for the time that you are at your peak of mental clarity so that you will create the most productive impression.

Make sure you arrive on time. Being late automatically creates a negative impression and can destroy the client's desire to deal with you. A small matter such as being late for an important appointment might represent an attitude and management style, which could cause conflict during the consulting project.

DURING THE INTERVIEW

The day has now arrived. You made certain you were at the client's office 10 to 15 minutes prior to the appointment so you had time to relax and compose yourself. You are feeling self-confident and positive about the meeting because you have thoroughly prepared yourself and worked through a mental role-play of events that are soon to occur.

Arriving early gives you an opportunity to observe the dynamics of the office and personnel and the general tone of the company. If you are going to have a relationship with a client, these simple factors are important to know beforehand.

When the meeting starts, it is important to shake hands with a firm grasp. A less than firm grasp will betray an insecure personality or lack of confidence in your abilities, and that impression alone could lose the project. It is important to consciously project a confident personality, positive attitude, firm method of speaking, and an attentive and relaxed stance. Exhibit a sense of control and leadership. A client wants to associate with a person who projects himself or herself well.

During the interview, you should spend almost all the time asking questions and little time answering them. After the initial social pleasantries and after you have briefly exchanged background information, control the meeting by asking your prepared questions. It is helpful to advise the client that you will be taking notes as this is a fact-finding interview. Having a prepared checklist is evidence of efficient administration. It also ensures that no questions will be overlooked, so interview consistency can be maintained.

Ask for examples to illustrate general statements. Ask open-ended, specific questions, and let the client do the talking. If a pause occurs, be prepared with the next question or other appropriate reaction. Listen intently to what the client says and how the client perceives the problem. If you want the client to continue elaborating on a situation, use questions starting with how, why, who, what, or where, or state, 'That's interesting, can you tell me more about that?'

Be aware of nonverbal communication in body posture, mannerisms, voice patterns, and behaviour. When forming an impression of a client's situation or opinion, restate it back to the client for confirmation.

If a client attempts to ask you a lot of questions, try to deflect the line of questioning back to the client. If the client asks specific questions about how you think the problem can be dealt with, or the various stages that should be considered, don't answer the questions directly. Your first interview is a fact-finding stage and you should not get involved in speculation or offering advice. Tell the client that you will certainly give an opinion later, after you have had an opportunity to review and analyse the facts and determine the options. Say that it would be premature and unprofessional for you to provide an opinion at the early stage. You don't want to give away free consulting, especially based on incomplete information.

At the end of the interview, ask the client if he or she would like to see a proposal and whether it should be a simple or detailed one.

Throughout the interview, be aware of the fears and concerns that might be present. Try to make sure you have dealt with all of them to the client's satisfaction.

AFTER THE INTERVIEW

Once the interview is over, you should review the data while it is still fresh in your mind. Identify the problems as you see them, and analyse the needs. Then outline the possible solutions and draft a proposal. The proposal steps are outlined in the next chapter.

The normal steps that follow include writing a thank-you letter to the client as soon as possible after the meeting and saying a proposal will follow as soon as it is complete.

WHY YOU SHOULD TURN DOWN BUSINESS

After your interview and assessment of the client, the project, and other factors involved, you may decide that it would be wise not to accept the project. That decision takes insight and foresight, and many consultants find it a difficult one to make. Consultants may be influenced by factors such as the need for cash flow; the challenge offered by the project; the potential marketing opportunities; the urge to do something when there are no other projects on the go; or the desire to help a client in need. Some of the reasons you should consider turning down business follow:

(a) A client looks as though he or she is on the verge of business failure. (Studies have shown that there are various reasons for business failure, including management incompetence, imbalanced experience, lack of management experience, or lack of experience in the product or service line. Some of the danger signals may include lack of a business plan, high overhead costs, low morale, lack of cash flow, lack of understanding of financial information, indecisiveness, backlog of commitments, inefficiency, poor communication, and general chaos. You do not want to be burdened with the stress of a client failure or the risk of not collecting your fee.)

(b) A client has a reputation for paying late or not at all.

(c) The client has a bad reputation for other reasons, and you do not want to be associated with that client.

(d) You do not like the client personally.

(e) A proposed project is illegal or unpleasant.

(f) You are overcommitted with other projects and unable to accept the work and perform satisfactorily and on time.

(g) The potential job is too small for your time, priorities, or cash flow.

(h) The potential job is too large for your ability or desire to administer it.

(i) You lack the expertise to perform the job to the standard that would be required.

(j) You do not offer consulting services in that client's field of operations.

(k) The client does not want to pay you the fee that you have requested, but wants to pay you less than you feel is fair to complete the project.

(l) The project would force you to compromise what you consider to be your professional and ethical standards.

(m) The client does not appear to fully appreciate your skills and abilities.

(n) The client does not have any money.

HOW TO TURN DOWN UNWANTED BUSINESS

Once you have decided that you do not want the business at all, or not in the form that it is available, there are various tactics and techniques to turn down the project in a way that maintains goodwill and does not hurt the client's feelings.

If the proposed project is simply unsuitable for you, you may wish to turn it down completely. There are different ways of rejecting projects directly:

(a) Tell the client that your present workload is very heavy and unfortunately you are unable to accept the job. This option makes you appear more attractive and desirable to the client for possible future projects.

(b) Tell the client you are unable to comply with the job specifications. This typically occurs with government agencies. If you are expected to take on a government contract because of previous projects, and you want to be considered favourably in the future, you could propose an approach that you feel the client will reject because it is outside the stated or unstated guidelines.

(c) Tell the client that you do not perform the particular type of service being requested, either because you do not have the capacity or it isn't your current field. If you normally perform that type of consulting, state that at the present time you are directing your talents and priorities in a slightly different direction.

(d) Bid the job too high. You can quote a fee much higher than you think the job is worth or that other competitors might bid. The risk here, of course, is that your bid might be accepted.

There may be occasions when you would accept a job if it was changed to meet your needs. Some of the techniques you could consider include:

(a) Accept only part of the proposed project. You could encourage other consultants to accept parts of the project you do not wish to handle.

(b) Redefine the project to meet your needs, and offer to conduct the assignment on your own terms. This approach works only if the client's goals, objectives, and expectations can be met without additional costs.

(c) Accept the job but act as project manager and employ other consultants to assist you in completing the work.

17

Consulting proposals

Most initial meetings result in a request for a proposal. The proposal plays a significant role in your ability to obtain consulting assignments. Because of the vital nature of writing and presenting successful proposals, you may wish to refer to appendix 3 for further references. This chapter covers some of the basic concepts and tactics required to produce successful proposals.

WHAT IS A PROPOSAL?

A proposal is a letter or document that you prepare for a client describing your understanding of the client's needs. This is very important because your client, in order to have confidence in you, must be satisfied that you understand the problem as well as he or she does.

The proposal states what you intend to do for the client and indicates in specific terms the anticipated results and potential benefits to the client.

A proposal is a selling document. It is intended to be informative and appealing and to convince the client to contract for your services.

PRIVATE VERSUS PUBLIC SECTOR PROPOSALS

Public sector proposals tend to be more formal than private sector proposals. When a client requests a proposal, the request is made on the assumption that anyone offering goods or services is properly qualified and equipped to do so. The government requires that you demonstrate your own competence and prove that your facilities, experience, resources, and whatever else are adequate to handle the requirements. The client is evaluating not only the merits of the programme you propose versus the merits of competitive programmes, but also your credentials versus the credentials of your competitors. It is common for government agencies to require that you outline your personal qualifications. One reason government agencies request such information is that they are required by procurement regulations to make an objective evaluation of each proposal. Your qualifications provide one specific comparison.

Private sector proposals are far more flexible in their selection requirements because they are not governed by legislation. Therefore, pragmatism and subjective factors have more of an influence on the final decision.

SOLICITED VERSUS UNSOLICITED PROPOSALS

Solicited proposals are proposals requested by a prospective client from the public or private sector. An organization requesting a proposal has already identified some needs. Your proposal will be judged on its quality, timeliness, reliability, and effectiveness.

An unsolicited proposal is designed by a consultant who perceives a need and is confident that it can be met through the use of the consultant's services.

Solicited proposals generally involve a competition between large numbers of consultants who bid on the project. In an unsolicited proposal situation, you may be the only person being considered.

SIMPLE AND FORMAL PROPOSALS

Simple proposal

The simple proposal is a written statement, typed on the consultant's stationery, that includes the following items:

(a) A description of the work to be done

(b) The name of the consultant performing the work

(c) The services or personnel to be provided by the client

(d) The date work will begin and the length of time required to complete the assignment

(e) An outline of anticipated categories of costs to be paid by the client

(f) The fees to be paid for services rendered and the terms arranged.

The proposal is signed by the consultant and normally sent by mail or delivered in person to the client. If the proposal is agreed upon, the client should sign a copy of the proposal or letter. The letter of proposal and agreement constitutes a legal contract and is similar to a letter of agreement.

Formal proposal

A formal proposal is considerably more detailed in that all aspects of the project are spelled out in full. It is similar to a formal contract and offers protection to both the consultant and the client.

The proposal does not become a legally binding contract until the client agrees to and signs the proposal document, until a covering letter referring to the proposal as a binding contract is signed, or until a formal contract is drafted reflecting the contents of the proposal and signed by both parties. A sample format for the formal proposal is described in the next section.

GUIDELINES AND FORMAT FOR A SUCCESSFUL PROPOSAL

The basis for your written contract will be the matters that you discuss at the proposal stage. Make sure you expand on the need, outcome, benefits, and results. Do not expand on the process or methods. This protects you from a client who might reject the proposal and perform the project in-house using your proposal as a guide or from a client who submits your proposal to other consultants for estimates and then hires someone else who uses the process you detailed.

Also keep in mind when you are preparing the proposal that your client might have some of the concerns and fears outlined in the preceding chapter. Attempt to minimize any concerns in the content of your proposal.

You should consider having a number of standardized proposals if there is similarity in the type of services you offer. If the standardized documents are on a computer, they can easily be adapted to include or exclude paragraphs and to make the document an original. It is also very easy to revise a document on a computer. The standardized proposal contains all the basics of any proposal, leaving open those items that are specific to each project. Another advantage of standardized proposals is your ability to deliver the completed proposal to the client within a short time after your initial meeting.

The sample proposal format (see Sample 16) is rather formal and detailed. It may include clauses that are not applicable or appropriate in all situations, as each project is unique. Delete the clauses that you do not need in your proposal – and be sure to renumber the clauses that remain!

PRESENTING YOUR PROPOSAL

How you package your proposal is nearly as important as how it is written. If possible, your proposal should be prepared on a computer as that reflects professionalism and quality resources. Your signature and the date should appear at the end of the proposal.

A covering letter accompanying your proposal should thank your client for his or her time and cooperation during the meeting and for the opportunity to submit a proposal. Highlight the topics discussed and state that you can help because you have had experience with this type of problem and would like to have the opportunity to be of service. You may want to flatter the client in some way by referring to his or her contribution in the meeting. Offer to answer any questions either by phone or at an arranged meeting. State that you will call within ten working days to discuss the proposal further. Put that date on your calendar. If you have not heard from the client within that period, make sure that you contact the client on the tenth day.

You may wish to suggest in your covering letter, if you didn't mention it in the proposal, that references are available upon request. You may wish to suggest that the client contact some of your other clients to discuss work you have performed. This should demonstrate your self-confidence and increase the client's trust and confidence in you.

PROPOSAL FOLLOW-UP

Your client may be slow in responding to your proposal. You do not want to appear to be pressuring the client, but you may have to take certain steps to clarify the situation or obtain a contract.

You stated in your covering letter that you would contact the client within ten working days. It is appropriate, then, that you do contact the client on the tenth day to answer any questions. You may receive further questions at that point, or obtain a positive or negative response to your proposal.

If the reason for the delay appears inexplicable, you may wish to wait for a further five business days and then drop in to see the client in person to ask if a decision has been made. This approach may or may not be appropriate in a given situation.

If a client is waiting for a committee decision, determine when the committee will meet to discuss the proposal and follow-up by phone to the client the day after the committee meets. You may also wish to consider giving an acceptance time limit in your proposal to encourage prompt consideration. In a given situation you might adopt the attitude that you would like to know one way or the other within a certain time. The client could construe the acceptance time limit in a positive fashion, as it could imply that you are in demand and may commit to other projects if the client does not book you in the allowed time.

SAMPLE 16
PROPOSAL FORMAT

1. TABLE OF CONTENTS: This should include headings and page numbers.

2. INTRODUCTION: It is important to persuade the client that you understand the project and the underlying factors that influence it. Briefly outline and analyse the factors that demonstrate the need. State that the matter is important and warrants professional outside assistance. Emphasize that you want to help and that you are the most appropriate source of help.

3. PROJECT PURPOSE: The purpose and goals of the engagement are outlined here in clear and accurate fashion. State the purpose and goals in the client's own words so that the client can identify with the proposal. During your initial interview you should have tried to find out what the client perceived as the needs or problems and the means to resolve them. Detail the goals in such a way that you can refer to them as specific and measurable outcomes so you have a reference point for measuring the progress of the project and satisfying the client.

4. PROJECT BENEFITS: Highlight the anticipated benefits the client will receive. Do not promise results you cannot guarantee, but keep in mind the client has to be given some realistic hope of success. This is a particularly important section as the client has to clearly understand and recognize the benefits in order to justify the financial and administrative commitment. Your client may have to account to other directors or shareholders. You assist your client to assist you by providing more detail.

5. APPROACH, SCOPE, AND PLAN: Compare and contrast several possible approaches to the project, if appropriate. Explain how you will proceed in general terms. Define the scope and limits of the proposed consulting service. Divide the tasks into smaller segments that provide clear stages in the project as reference points for you and your client. As mentioned earlier, provide sufficient information to demonstrate your competence, but not enough about the process and techniques to provide a formula for the client to perform the project without you.

6. PROJECT SCHEDULE: Determine the schedule and list the specific tasks required to attain the objectives. State the timing sequence of tasks according to the various stages. A bar chart or flow diagram might help to graphically assist the client's understanding and provide a reference point for progress.

7. PROGRESS REPORTS: It is important to maintain continual communication with the client. As explained in earlier chapters, the more information you provide your client, the more confidence the client will have in you and the less risk there is of problems occurring. Progress reports are frequently made at specific stages, when interim bills are sent. A client is more disposed to pay if tangible benefits can be seen and specific problems have been resolved. The frequency and format of periodic progress reports should be specified.

SAMPLE 16 *(Continued)*

8. COSTING SUMMARY: Explain your fees, types of fee arrangement, invoicing procedures, and timing of invoices. Detail the expected expenses that will be passed on directly to the client. Your client should understand that your estimate for time and costs is an estimate only. Provide sufficient detail about your fees so that your client appreciates the correlation between the amount of time expended and the cost of your services. Outline any other terms and conditions or variables that could affect the final cost.

9. PERSONNEL AND QUALIFICATIONS: Provide a brief background history of your firm and the personnel who will be consulting on the project. If you have had experience solving problems similar to the client's, make reference to that. Select only those aspects of your background experience that relate directly to the client and the proposal.

10. SUBCONTRACTS: If you are subcontracting or collaborating with other consultants, it is important to specify who they are and what duties they will perform. To avoid any future problems, specify whether you or the client is responsible for their technical performance.

11. USE OF CLIENT PERSONNEL: It is important that the client understand what commitments and obligations will be his or her responsibility. If you are to delegate responsibilities or otherwise receive assistance from the client's staff or executives, you should make it clear that your fee estimate is based on the use of client personnel. Specify personnel duties and time required if possible.

12. SENIOR MANAGEMENT SUPPORT: Make the executives aware that their support is vital to the success of the project. It is important that support for the project be communicated throughout the organization to gain cooperation and compliance. If regular meetings are going to be held with senior executives, specify the purpose and frequency of such meetings.

13. STEERING COMMITTEE FUNCTION, IF APPLICABLE: A steering committee reviews, coordinates, assists, and implements the consultant's work. It provides momentum, organizational credibility, and decision-making functions for the project. Detail the purposes, composition, and responsibilities of this committee.

14. OUTPUT MATERIAL INCLUDED: Describe any reports, surveys, instructional material, or other products that are part of the proposal.

15. MANAGEMENT PLAN: Describe your approach to managing the overall project. Who will be the client contact person, and what will his or her management role and authority be pertaining to the project?

16. DISCLAIMERS: If you have used disclaimers regarding the project, make sure that the reason is outlined. Your role is strictly that of adviser, not decision-maker, and any benefits achieved are based on both your recommendations and the client's actions and decisions. If your client does not fulfil his or her obligations and support, your responsibility and

SAMPLE 16 *(Continued)*

choices should be outlined. Indicate who has ownership and control over any proprietary information that could develop from your services, for example instructional material.

17. REFERENCES: If requested, or if it is your style and wish to provide client references, make sure that you obtain written permission in advance from the clients. Contact references occasionally to make sure they still think highly of you.

18. SUMMARY AND CLOSE OF PROPOSAL: This should be a short restatement of your belief in the importance of the engagement. Mention your availability to answer questions. If you are prepared to begin the project within a short time after the client's acceptance, state that clearly. You want to stimulate the client's need and persuade the client that you can fulfil the need.

WHAT TO DO IF YOUR PROPOSAL IS NOT ACCEPTED

It is helpful if you can determine why you received a rejection. Budget restraints, other priorities, or lack of consensus could be reasons. Possibly another consultant was awarded the contract. If possible, find out who obtained the assignment and why that proposal was selected over your own. Rejected proposals can provide a good learning experience. However, it may not be appropriate, practical, or possible for you to obtain the answer from the client.

Regardless of the circumstances, write a thank-you letter to the client expressing your appreciation for his or her time, interest, and cooperation, and mention that you would be pleased to submit a proposal for consideration in any future projects.

HOW TO AVOID GIVING AWAY FREE CONSULTING

At this stage you should know whether your proposal was rejected or accepted. If it was rejected, you may have provided too much information in your proposal to your client. The client, in turn, may have used the information for his or her benefit. In other words, you gave away free consulting. If your proposal was accepted and you now have a contract or a contract is being prepared, you should be aware of the various ways that clients can innocently or intentionally obtain your advice for free.

Occasionally, you may decide to share your knowledge and ideas in an attempt to build goodwill with the client or prospective client. That is a judgement you will have to make at the time. But you are running a business, which requires income and profit. You cannot carelessly give away the only product you have, which is time and skill.

Potential client interview or discussion

A potential client may contact you and wish to discuss ideas and problems with you on the telephone, over lunch, or at the client's office or your office. The potential client wants to 'pick your brains.' You willingly cooperate due to your desire to obtain a consulting assignment.

The strategic solution is to confirm that you do provide service in the area concerned and you are available to the client on a professional basis and would be pleased to establish a relationship. Answer any concerns raised by the client by asking questions aimed at drawing out information. Do not offer solutions but imply that there are solutions to the problems discussed.

If answers are specifically requested, respond that you require far more information before providing an answer. State that it would be unprofessional for you to provide an opinion without sufficient information on which to base that opinion. Again, restate that you would be pleased to discuss the matter further on a professional basis if the client so wishes.

These deflective techniques are the same ones outlined in the preceding chapter relating to the initial interview. Ask the client directly if he or she is interested in retaining a consultant to provide assistance in the specific area of concern. Clarify if the client would like you to submit a proposal to resolve the problem. Decide if the client is a serious enough prospect to spend the time on a proposal.

Make it clear throughout the discussion that you are paid for professional services and that you are capable of assisting the client on a fee for service basis.

Analysis of client's need

A client might perceive that a problem exists, but does not understand the precise nature of the problem. The client implies that if you analyse the need and make recommendations for resolution, an attractive contract could immediately result. This teaser can entice unsophisticated or new consultants to provide a thorough diagnosis without fee.

A naive consultant can be easily exploited by a person using this technique. The risk, of course, is that no subsequent contracts materialize or some other consultant is retained. One way of resolving this problem is to recommend that the client enter into a contract with a first stage that is a diagnostic stage. After the diagnosis is made, with recommendations, then the consultant could proceed to the next stage of the contract and implement the recommendations. In this way the consultant is protected by contract and the sincerity of the client is assured.

An option can be inserted in the contract stating that if the client elects not to proceed with the recommendation, then the consultant is assured of payment of an agreed sum in consideration for the time and energies spent during the diagnosis.

Free detailed advice in the written proposal

In your proposal you may write a complete, detailed formula with all the necessary instructions together with an outline of the methods and steps required to attain the objective. The client now has the prescription for resolving the problem and can give it to other consultants to submit an estimate or can implement the detailed proposal with in-house personnel.

You can avoid this problem by writing a proposal that highlights in detail the need that exists, the objectives that must be achieved to resolve the client's problem, and the measurable, specific outcomes and benefits that will be attained at specific stages of the assignment. A functional flow diagram graphically illustrating the steps is an effective marketing tool. Do not include detailed information on the processes or methods to be used.

Potential future benefit

A client may try to convince you that some future benefit, such as goodwill or contacts, could occur if you perform the service, on the condition that you provide the service for free or a reduced amount as the price to pay for future opportunities.

This technique is normally exercised by larger or more influential clients who take advantage of a consultant's impressionable, desperate, or opportunistic nature. The client may attempt to blame the lack of financial recompense on budget allocations having been spent, internal financial restraints being imposed, or a general hold on all project commitments. From a consultant's viewpoint, the mere association with an influential or prestigious client could be an inducement.

As long as you are aware of the business and psychological dynamics at work, you can make a responsible, pragmatic decision. The decision might be to accede to the client's overtures, resist them, or attempt to negotiate a more realistic package.

Additions to the original fixed price contract

It is not uncommon for a client to request additional work outside the original contract terms, as all needs cannot be foreseen in advance or changing circumstances can change the needs. Once you are aware that the request is outside the fixed price contract terms, you should contact the client, draw this fact to the client's attention in a polite fashion, and suggest that a modified contract or addendum be negotiated to incorporate the additional work.

This situation reinforces the importance of being specific in the fixed price contract as to the services that are to be performed. Ambiguity in terms could lead to a difference of opinion, an impasse, legal problems, and loss of goodwill as well as loss of a client.

Depending on the circumstances, a formal contract amendment may not be required; a confirmation letter outlining the amendments and signed by both parties may be enough. The method is a matter of style, nature of client, and other circumstances.

Free consulting in a follow-up situation

You can run into problems when you have performed your services as outlined in your contract, but the client continues to need your services for operating the project. For example, suppose you recommended a type of computer hardware that was subsequently installed in the client's premises, and the client's personnel had difficulty learning the new equipment. You might feel an obligation to assist the client by explaining the necessary matters to the personnel. You may then be continually phoned by the client who requests you to return to explain various features to the personnel. Unless you are aware this process is occurring, you could be providing considerable free consulting.

The obvious solution is to anticipate the situation and incorporate provisions for follow-up consultation fees into the original contract. The contract can specify the method and terms of payment. One option is a retainer contract, which means that you perform a specified service regularly (e.g., several specified hours or days per month). Another option is an availability or call-off contract. This means you are 'on call' for a fixed monthly fee as outlined in the terms of the agreement.

Relatives, associates, and friends

Relatives and friends may frequently come to you for advice. You must develop ways to maintain the relationship while clarifying your role as a professional who provides service for a fee.

You can develop various subtle but effective approaches. One technique is to say that you have a policy of not advising family or friends because of possible conflict of interest or bias. Because you value the relationship and operate by professional standards, you feel it would not be appropriate or responsible, and you would prefer not to provide professional advice that they might rely on.

Another approach is to say you are unable to provide advice because of incomplete information, and it would be irresponsible, unprofessional, and unfair on your part to give an opinion based on incomplete facts.

You have choices. You can either decline to provide advice, provide advice for free, or establish your relationship in the context as a business one and negotiate a fee for service. It is also helpful to keep in mind that you can be exposed to professional liability and negligence claims if your advice is followed and problems occur, even though you did not charge or get paid for your advice.

18

Contracts

As a consultant, you will quickly become aware of the necessity for written contracts in all your business and client relationships. A contract is the framework within which your obligations, rights, remedies, and remunerations are clarified. There are oral, written, and implied contracts. You want to make sure that your consulting business assumes no commitments or financial outlay without the security of an agreement in writing. Many consultants and other small business people commence their business with the trusting attitude that a verbal agreement is sufficient. It only takes one bad experience to demonstrate the folly of relying on a verbal agreement. This chapter explores some of the important aspects of contracts.

ESSENTIALS OF A VALID CONTRACT

A contract is an agreement between two parties to perform mutual obligations. The most common forms of contract are the oral contract and the written contract. The problem with an oral contract is that if the parties disagree, unless there are reliable witnesses or part performance of the agreement, it is difficult to reconstruct what the original bargain was. A written contract simply records in a formal or informal manner the nature of the bargain. For example, if you send a letter to a client confirming your agreement, and if the five essential elements of a contract are present, you have a simple informal contract.

The five elements of a contract are as follows:

Offer

If you submit a proposal or a contract to a client, it constitutes your offer to the client to accept your proposal. Your offer, naturally, will be in writing and will spell out the particulars in some detail.

Acceptance

Acceptance of your proposal must be clearly demonstrated. Normally this takes the form of your prospective client confirming in writing his or her acceptance of your proposal letter or document or contract, and acknowledging the terms you have outlined.

In certain situations an acceptance can be assumed and the contract made valid by part performance. In other words, it could be argued that your offer was accepted if your client permitted you to perform in part or in full the terms of your written proposal, even though a written acceptance had not been received. Naturally, this is a high-risk manner of doing business. Never begin a project without first protecting yourself in writing.

Consideration

Consideration is something of value being promised to you or given to you in exchange for your services. Valuable consideration normally refers to money or some other valuable assets, but a promise to pay money or provide some other benefit can be deemed to be consideration.

Competency

An agreement will not be considered binding if signed by persons lacking competence to understand the 'nature and quality of their actions.' This includes minors, the mentally infirm, or a person who was intoxicated at the time the agreement was accepted or signed. The age at which a person ceases to become a minor varies depending on the jurisdiction. In some circumstances a contract signed by a minor is considered to be binding.

Legality

A contract created to perform an illegal act is void. For example, if a number of businesses signed an agreement to fix prices in their area of product sales, and one of the parties failed to follow the agreement, the other parties to the agreement would not be able to sue for breach of contract as the subject matter of the agreement was illegal.

WHY A WRITTEN CONTRACT IS NEEDED

There are many reasons why a written contract is essential. Some of the reasons are listed below:

▌ *Project professional image:* A written contract enhances your image as a responsible professional and businessperson.

▌ *Avoid misunderstandings:* It is difficult to remember complex details without having them in writing. Subsequent events and distractions can cloud your recall of earlier conversations. Both parties can have differing assumptions and interpretations of what was agreed on critical points of issue. It only makes sense to prevent this problem by the simple act of writing down the agreement.

▌ *Untruthful client:* It is not uncommon with verbal agreements for one party to reconstruct the agreement in a self-serving fashion at some later point. This could be to negotiate a more favourable contract or to get out of the contract obligations altogether. If it is just one person's word against another's, it is difficult if not impossible for a court to reconstruct with certainty the original bargain. The time, delay, and expense of attempting to assert your rights eliminates the profit and possibly your business as well.

▌ *Death of either party:* If either party to an unwritten contract dies, the estate of the deceased would have difficulty determining the actual bargain. This could give rise to lawsuits against the estate of the deceased consultant if the client claimed damages had been suffered due to breach of contract because of the death. The estate of the deceased would be in a difficult position to defend any action, not knowing the exact terms and obligations of both parties.

▌ *Terms of payment outlined:* If you do not have specific terms of payment (ie, payment each month or at specific stages in the project) in writing, the client could attempt to wait until the end of the job to pay, claiming there was no other agreement to the contrary. You want to avoid this problem by having a written agreement before you expend your time, energy, and resources.

▌ *Fee for service confirmed:* You want to make clear that you are being paid for your time and that your efforts are not being supplied free as a marketing device or preliminary assessment.

▌ *Avoid and limit liability:* You want to protect your interests in writing by having provisions in the agreement to protect yourself from liability. For example, you may want to have a contingency clause to the effect that if events occur outside your control, you are not to be held responsible. You might also consider a limited liability clause that sets a fixed amount of money that you would be responsible for if you are held liable.

▌ *Prevent litigation:* If you do not have an agreement in writing, a client could claim that you acted improperly or that the work was not completely done. Unless an agreement in writing spelled out the nature of the services that you were going to provide, it would be difficult for you or your client to show exactly what you agreed upon. Because of this impasse on the terms and obligations of the agreement, litigation might be difficult to avoid.

▋ *Collateral for financing:* A written contract outlining benefits that you will receive for performing services is as good as money. You can pledge the contract at a bank as security for loan advances. This ability to lever your legal documents for working capital or cash flow purposes is just good business sense. No banker will lend money on the strength of your verbal assurance that you have a consulting agreement with a client.

▋ *Potential for increase of revenue:* If you have a contract that details the exact services and supplies you are providing, any variation will allow you to negotiate an addendum to the agreement. With an oral agreement, there could be a dispute over the exact point at which your services and supplies are not included in the bargain.

▋ *Independent contractor status confirmed:* Without a written agreement specifying your independent status of operating, within the terms of the agreement, without direction or control, you could be considered to be an employee by the tax authorities. Make clear in the written agreement the nature of the roles of the parties. Also, the client might set down his or her own specifications, or question you in detail on an ongoing basis about what you are doing, thereby reducing some of your independence. To prevent this, take the initiative to specify the detail, nature, and form of the services you are going to provide.

▋ *Encourage contract acceptance:* Many prospective clients feel nervous about agreeing to have you perform a project unless they know the exact detail and terms of the relationship in writing. The person with whom you might be negotiating frequently has to explain the particulars to colleagues or superiors. Without a written contract in writing, you might not win the assignment.

▋ *Communication:* As mentioned previously, good communication is an essential ingredient for client satisfaction and goodwill. A well-written contract helps build client confidence.

STRUCTURE OF FORMAL CONTRACT

A consulting contract can vary widely in its complexity depending on the nature and value of the project being performed and the clients being served. Sample 17 describes the format for a formal contract and discusses clauses that are frequently included. Not all the clauses are necessarily appropriate or applicable in each case. A simple contract or letter of understanding does not need the same detail.

SAMPLE 17

CONTRACT FORMAT

1. PARTIES INVOLVED: Name all parties involved in the contract and state the date the contract is signed.

2. TERM OF CONTRACT: The starting and completion dates of the contract are written here, or a reference is made to an appendix in which the dates and hours are described. The contract may state either the beginning and ending dates of an assignment, or both, or a maximum of hours within a fixed time period. The time period can either be closed or open. An open contract simply states that a specific job is to be performed, without giving a deadline for completion. Or a contract might simply state that an ongoing relationship is commencing, the length of which shall be at the pleasure of both parties.

3. DUTIES OF THE CONSULTANT: Outline your proposed consulting in detail, by specific task and scope. In previous meetings during the proposal stage you have probably clarified services to be offered, and the proposal letter or document spells out what you are offering. If this is included in the contract for practical, tactical, or legal reasons, or choice of style, the following areas might be covered:

    ▌ Services that you, as consultant, will provide

    ▌ The timing of the submission of various documents pertaining to the project

    ▌ The nature of reports to be furnished, if any, and the approximate dates when they will be completed

    ▌ Any special materials to be prepared, such as brochures, etc.

    ▌ The timing and nature of any consultant/client meetings, either on fixed dates or at specific stages in the project or upon mutual request

    ▌ Travel that might be required, the nature of compensation, when that is to be paid, and what is required to obtain payment

    ▌ Your authority to use client resources, office equipment, computer, files and records, and access to client's customers

    ▌ Your right to use third party information; for example ledgers and journals and other financial information in the possession of the client

    ▌ A provision restricting you from performing services for the client's competitors (Be careful of this provision, especially if you intend to develop a clientele base within a certain industry.)

4. DUTIES OF THE CLIENT: Wherever a consultant requires access to information or to employees, customers, or advisers of the client, it should be specified clearly in the agreement that the client agrees and will have the

SAMPLE 17 (*Continued*)

responsibility of facilitating and performing in those specified areas. For example, if you require information from a third party, you should try to have the client responsible for obtaining the information for you. If the client does not or cannot cooperate and therefore impedes the project, how will you be compensated?

5. PAYMENT FOR SERVICES: This is an important section and should state the basis on which your fees will be paid; i.e., per diem, fixed rate, fixed price plus expenses, or another form. Various types of fee structures are discussed in chapter 13. When and how the invoices will be rendered should be spelled out clearly; for example, invoices could be rendered at specific identifiable stages throughout the project. If the client is being invoiced on an hourly or daily rate, that rate should be specified in the contract. If a down payment (retainer) is required, that should also be specified.

6. EXPENSES: Any job-related expenses to be paid by the client are described here. In the case of a fixed price contract, your expenses are incorporated in the fixed price agreed upon. Most other forms of fee structure involve expenses to be paid by the client. Outline what is required for payment.

7. LATE PAYMENT: The contract should specify when a payment should take place – either at specified periods, upon receipt of invoice, 30 days after invoice, or whatever arrangement is agreed upon. A clause can be inserted in the agreement stating that if the invoice is not paid within the agreed upon billing period, interest on the overdue account will be added. The interest rate is normally slightly higher than the prevailing bank rate, which acts as an incentive to pay.

8. STOP WORK CLAUSE: This clause allows the consultant to cease providing services on the project until the outstanding fees and interest have been paid. Generally this clause is not applied until a certain period has elapsed and all other attempts at getting payment through goodwill have been unsuccessful. Stopping work is a last resort. It is important that the basis on which you can discontinue your services be stated in the contract.

9. INDEPENDENT CONTRACTOR: State that you are an independent contractor and therefore not eligible to participate in any benefit programmes or tax withholding obligations on the part of the client. This clause makes it clear that you are not an employee.

10. WORK DELEGATION: Outline the basis on which you are permitted to hire assistants and delegate work. Depending upon the nature of services you are providing, your personal service and expertise is probably desired by the client. If you plan to subcontract out to other people, protect yourself by clarifying that in the contract.

11. ADDITIONAL WORK: This clause allows a client to request a modification to the contract and add a provision for additional services. Any modification to the contract should be confirmed in writing with particulars and signed by both parties before any additional service work commences.

SAMPLE 17 (Continued)

12. CONFIDENTIALITY: State that any information disclosed to you pertaining to the project or any information that you become aware of during the period of the project will be kept strictly confidential.

13. OWNERSHIP: This clause covers ownership of materials or ideas resulting from your services. Many rejected ideas and plans could be useful for another project. Naturally, it is not in your best interests to have the client own this information. You should require that rejected plans or ideas are to remain your property.

14. LIMITED LIABILITY OF THE CONSULTANT: You may wish to insert a clause saying any liability that is the result of your mistakes or breach of contract is limited to the amount of the contract price, assuming that there is a fixed contract price, or the amount of loss, whichever is lower. If there is no fixed contract price, set a specific maximum to the loss. However, such a clause is difficult if not impossible to enforce. You should also take out professional liability insurance and errors and omissions insurance as a protection (see chapter 11).

15. CONTINGENCIES: This clause states that you have complete control of all services rendered, with the exception of events beyond the control of you or the client such as accidents, delays, strikes, or supplier problems. This 'force majeure' clause attempts to protect both parties if the contract cannot be completed.

16. ADVERTISING: This clause restricts the use of the client's name for media release without the written approval of the client.

17. ARBITRATION: Outline the procedures to be followed in the event of disagreement by either party about the terms or interpretation of the terms of the contract. Normally, provision is made for a dispute to be settled by an independent arbitrator, with details about the basis on which the arbitrator will be paid and by whom, and the criteria for selecting the arbitrator.

18. GOVERNING LAWS: This clause simply states that the contract shall be governed by the laws of the jurisdiction in which it is written.

19. TERMINATION: Either party is allowed to terminate services upon written notification a set number of days in advance. Outline the details and the reasons under which termination can take place.

20. AGREEMENT BINDING: State that the written agreement is the total agreement between the parties and shall take the place of any previous contracts or verbal or written agreements. This clause normally states that any modification to the agreement must be in writing and agreed between the parties to be enforceable.

21. SIGNATURES: The parties to the contract sign the agreement. It is very important that the client representative who signs has the authority to do so and that his or her position is written on the contract. In some cases, corporate seals are required if corporations are involved.

If a proposal letter or document exists, it can be referred to in the contract as part of the agreement and attached as an appendix.

TYPES OF CONTRACT

There are several types of contract frequently used in the consulting business. It is important to understand the options that are available to you as they involve various tactical and legal considerations. Following is a brief summary of the most common types of contract.

Letter of agreement

This simple contract is in the form of a letter stating a summary of the agreement between the parties. This includes the nature of services to be performed, the method and time of payment, the starting date and duration of the contract, the resource materials and personnel to be supplied by the client, if applicable, and the consultants who will be involved on the project, if applicable.

The letter of agreement is normally prepared by the consultant and forwarded to the client for signature and approval. An example of a letter of agreement prepared by a consultant is shown in Sample 18.

Sample 19 shows a letter of agreement prepared by the client. Note the differences in tone and format between the two. The one prepared by the client has the appearance of a short formal contract.

Letter of agreement with general terms and conditions appended

Another option is to have a letter of agreement accompanied by a statement of standard terms and conditions (see Sample 20). The statement is a standardized form that you can use often for similar type of agreements. It covers matters such as fee structure, reimbursable expenses, subcontracts, invoices and payments, warranty, and limitation of professional liability. Other clauses can be included in this form based on your own needs and precautions. If you prefer this format, the letter of agreement attached to the terms and conditions need not be detailed. It can outline the specific, not general, terms of the agreement.

The letter of agreement and/or general terms and conditions form are frequently used if the client does not want a more formal contract. From a tactical viewpoint, you might use these if you feel that a client would be intimidated by a formally structured contract. Another factor might be your personal style of consulting practice. If the contract is not complex and the fee is low, you might favour the simpler contract format.

SAMPLE 18

LETTER OF AGREEMENT

(PREPARED BY CONSULTANT)

(Consultant's letterhead)

_____ 20 _____

Mary Roberts
Chief Executive
ABC Ltd
10 London Road
Any town, Anywhere
Dear _____

Re: Consulting Agreement

This letter will confirm our understanding concerning the terms of retainer and nature of services to be performed for ABC Ltd. These terms are as follows:

1. Term. This agreement will be for a period of _____ commencing on _____. Either of us may terminate this agreement within thirty (30) days' written notice to the other party. In the event of termination, I will be compensated for services rendered up to the date of termination.

2. Duties. My duties will include:
   (a) Review, analysis and recommendations for changes in the systems and organizational structure of the research division.
   (b) Preparation of weekly reports on the progress of the project.
   (c) Preparation of a final report and oral presentation for the management of the company, with recommendations for implementing system and organizational improvements and related costing.

3. Fee. The fee for my services shall be at the rate of £750 per day, payable on receipt as invoiced. Other out-of-pocket costs, such as travel expenses and secretarial services, will be invoiced separately at cost.

Enclosed is a copy of this agreement for your records. Please sign the original and return it to this office in the enclosed envelope. If you have any questions, please contact me.

Yours sincerely,

David Jones
Consultant

Accepted and agreed to:

_____   _____
                                                    Date

SAMPLE 19
LETTER OF AGREEMENT
(PREPARED BY CLIENT)

ABC Ltd
10 London Road
Anytown, Anywhere

_____ 20 ____

Smith Jones & Associates
Consultants
20 High Street
Anytown, Anywhere
Dear _____,

Re: Consulting Project

I am pleased to announce that your proposal to ABC Ltd has been accepted. The conditions of our acceptance are outlined below.

1. **Term**. Your appointment as a consultant to ABC Ltd (hereinafter called 'the Company') is confirmed for the period ____ to ____.

2. **Services.** You shall perform such work or services as are set forth in Exhibit A, attached hereto and specifically made a part of this Agreement. The work or services to be performed by you may be changed by the Company from time to time by letter requests sent to you. You shall keep the Company informed on the progress of any work being performed under this Agreement.

3. **Fees and expenses.**

    (a) The Company will pay you a total fee of £____ for all work performed hereunder on satisfactory completion of the work.

    (b) Your fee will be at the rate of £____ per month for all work performed hereunder. You will be paid at the same time you are reimbursed for approved expenses under paragraph 3(c) below.

    (c) You will receive reimbursement for the actual cost of reasonable expenses arising out of the work performed under this Agreement (not to exceed £____), subject to the approval of the Company. You shall deliver an itemized statement to the Company on a monthly basis that shows fully the work being performed under this Agreement and all related expenses. The Company will pay you at the amount of any authorized expenses within thirty (30) days of the receipt of the item-ized statement of all expenses, submitted together with receipts for all hotel, car rental, air fare and other transportation expenses for all other expenses of £20 or more.

SAMPLE 19 (*Continued*)

4. **Working facilities.** You will be furnished with such facilities and services as shall be suitable for your position and adequate for the performance of your duties under this Agreement.

5. **Reports.** Any and all reports, manuscripts and any other work products, whether completed or not, that are prepared or developed by you as part of the work under this Agreement shall be the property of the Company and shall be turned over to the Company promptly at the Company's request or at the termination of this Agreement, whichever is earlier.

6. **Independent contractor.** You shall exercise control over the means and manner in which you perform any work requested hereunder, and in all respects your relationship to the Company shall be that of an independent contractor serving as a consultant and not as an employee.

7. **Termination.** This Agreement may be terminated upon thirty (30) days' written notice by either party.

8. **Confidential information.** You agree that, for the term of your appointment hereunder and for two (2) years thereafter, you will not disclose to any person, firm or corporation any confidential information regarding the Company, its business, directors, officers and employees.

9. **Non-assignable.** This agreement is personal in nature and is not assignable by you or by the Company.

10. **Entire agreement.** This letter, including Exhibit A, contains the entire agreement of the parties. It may not be changed orally but only by an agreement signed by the party against whom enforcement of any waiver, change, modification, extension or discharge is sought.

I trust that the terms of this appointment meet with your approval. If so, please indicate this by signing a copy of this letter and returning it to the Company. An additional copy of this letter is enclosed for your records.

Yours sincerely,

_____
Client signature

Accepted and agreed to this _____ day of _____, 20 _____

_____
Consultant signature

SAMPLE 20

STATEMENT OF GENERAL TERMS AND CONDITIONS

1. Fee structure

All time, including travel hours, spent on the project by professional personnel will be invoiced. The following approximate ranges of hourly rates for various categories of personnel are currently in effect.

Category	Hourly rate
Principal	£100
Consultant	£75

Hourly rates are liable to be adjusted as necessary to reflect inflation. Three months' notice will be given before any such fee adjustment. Unless otherwise stated, any cost estimate presented in a proposal is for budgetary purposes only, and is not a fixed price. The budget figure will not be exceeded without prior authorization from the client.

2. Reimbursable expenses

The following expenses will be invoiced at cost:

(a) Travel expenses necessary for the execution of the project, including air fares, rented vehicles and road mileage in company or personal vehicles, which will be charged at 32p per mile (this sum will be reviewed every six months). Air travel will be by business class, where available

(b) Telephone charges

(c) Postage

(d) Printing and reproduction

(e) Computer services, including word processing

(f) Other expenses directly attributable to the project.

3. Invoices and payments

Invoices will be submitted monthly and payment is due on receipt of invoice. Rates for foreign contracts are negotiable and the above rates do not apply.

4. Warranty

Our professional services will be performed, our findings obtained and our recommendations prepared in accordance with generally and currently accepted management consulting principles and practices. The warranty is in lieu of all other warranties either expressed or implied.

5. Other documents

(eg Proposal letter dated _____) is hereby made a part of this document.

SAMPLE 20 *(Continued)*

6. **Acceptance by client**

Client, by signing below, hereby agrees to these general terms and conditions of Client except as noted below:

CLIENT (typed name of client)

BY: _____

(Signature)
(Name and designation)

SAMPLE 21

FORMAL CONSULTING CONTRACT

ABC & Company (hereinafter called 'the Company') desires to use the expert assistance of _____ (hereinafter called 'the Consultant') in the fields in which the Consultant has professional qualifications.

1. **Parties and relationships**

   The Company is engaged in the business of consulting and the provision of technical assistance and training to small business through the use of skilled independent contractors. The Consultant is a person who by education, training and experience is skilled in the provision of the service required.

2. **Character and extent of services**

   (a) It is the mutual intent of the parties that the Consultant shall act strictly in a professional consulting capacity as an independent contractor for all purposes and in all situations and shall not be considered an employee of the Company.

   (b) The Consultant reserves full control of his activities to the manner and selection methods with respect to rendering his professional consulting services to the Company.

   (c) The Consultant agrees to perform his activities in accordance with the highest and best state of the art of his professionalism.

3. **Period of service and termination**

   (a) The period of service by the Consultant under this Agreement shall be from _____ to _____ and may be renewed upon the mutual agreement of the parties hereto.

   (b) Either the Company or the Consultant may terminate this Agreement by giving the other party thirty (30) days' written notice of intention and such action.

   (c) The Company reserves the right to halt or terminate the conduct of a seminar/workshop by the Consultant without prior notice or claim for additional compensation should, in the opinion of the Company, such conduct not be in the best interests of the Company.

4. **Fees**

   (a) Upon the Consultant's acceptance hereof, the Company agrees to pay the Consultant according to the following schedule:

   (Insert fee rate or fixed fee and any allowance for or schedule of allowable expenses, if any.)

   (b) In the event that the Company desires, and it is mutually agreed to by the Consultant, the Consultant's services may be used in the conduct of training/consulting programmes not specifically identified in para-

SAMPLE 21 (*Continued*)

graph 4(a). In such cases, the Company agrees to pay the Consultant on the basis of the following schedule:

(Insert fee or fixed fee and any allowance for or schedule of allowable expenses, if any.)

(c)   In the event of special circumstances, variations to the fee schedule of paragraphs 4(a) and 4(b) will be allowed as mutually agreed to in writing by the parties hereto.

5.   **Notification**

The Consultant will be notified by the Company in writing to begin his participation in specific training and/or consultation assignments to which the fee schedule of paragraphs 4(a) and 4(b) applies. Such notification will include a statement of the time(s) and place(s) of the intended training/consultation involvement with other necessary information.

6.   **Expenses**

The Consultant, as an independent contractor, shall be responsible for any expenses incurred in the performance of this Agreement, except as otherwise agreed to in writing prior to such expenses being incurred. The Company will reimburse the Consultant for reasonable travel expenses incurred with respect hereto.

(A specification of 'reasonable' may be inserted here.)

7.   **Method**

(a)   The Consultant shall be paid as provided for in paragraphs 4(a) and 4(b) hereof, on the basis of a properly executed 'Claim for Consulting Service' form (sample attached).

(b)   The 'Claim for Consulting Service' form is to be submitted at the end of the calendar month during which consulting services are performed. Exceptions to this arrangement are allowed with the written approval of the Company.

(c)   Payment to the Consultant will be made by cheque, despatched not later than _____ days subsequent to receipt of the 'Claim for Consulting Service' form as provided for in paragraphs 7(a) and 7(b).

8.   **Copyrights**

(a)   The Consultant agrees that the Company shall determine the disposition of the title to and the rights under any copyright secured by the Consultant or his employee on copyrightable material first produced or composed and delivered to the Company under this Agreement. The Consultant hereby grants to the Company a royalty free, non-exclusive, irrevocable licence to reproduce, translate, publish, use and dispose of, and to authorize others to do so, all copyrighted or copyrightable work not first produced or composed by the Consultant

SAMPLE 21 (*Continued*)

in the performance of this Agreement but which is incorporated into the material furnished under this Agreement, provided that such licence shall be only to the extent the Consultant now has or prior to the completion or final settlement of this Agreement may acquire the right to grant such licence without becoming liable to pay compensation to others solely because of such grant.

(b) The Consultant agrees that he will not knowingly include any copyrighted material in any written or copyrightable material furnished or delivered under this Agreement without a licence as provided in paragraph 8(a) hereof or without the consent of the copyright owner, unless specific written approval of the Company to the inclusion of such copyrighted material is secured.

(c) The Consultant agrees to report in writing to the Company promptly and in reasonable detail any notice or claim of copyright infringement received by the Consultant with respect to any material delivered under this Agreement.

9. **Drawings, designs, specifications**

(a) All drawings, sketches, designs, design data, specifications, notebooks, technical and scientific data, and all photographs, negatives, reports, findings, recommendations, data and memoranda of every description relating thereto, as well as all copies foregoing, relating to the work performed under this Agreement or any part thereof, shall be subject to the inspection of the Company at all reasonable times; and the Consultant and his employees shall afford the Company proper facilities for such inspection; and further shall be the property of the Company and may be used by the Company for any purpose whatsoever without any claim on the part of the Consultant and his employees for additional compensation, and subject to the right of the Consultant to retain a copy of said material shall be delivered to the Company or otherwise disposed of by the Consultant, either as the Company may from time to time direct during the process of work, or in any event, as the Company shall direct upon the completion or termination of this Agreement.

10. **Confidentiality**

(a) It is understood that in the performance of his duties, the Consultant will obtain information about both the Company and the Company's client, and that such information may include financial data, client lists, methods of operating, policy statements and other confidential data.

(b) The Consultant agrees to restrict his use of such above-mentioned information to the performance of duties described in this Agreement. The Consultant further agrees to return to the Company and to the Company's client upon the completion of his duties any and all documents (originals

SAMPLE 21 *(Continued)*

and copies) taken from either organization to facilitate the project described herein.

11. **Noncompetition**

    The Consultant agrees that he will not perform his professional services for any organization known to the Consultant to be a client of the Company unless the Company has employed the Consultant for the provision of such services to the client. This restriction shall remain in effect for a period of two years after the termination of this Agreement. For the purposes of this section, 'client' is defined as any organization which, during the said period of restriction, has engaged the Company to promote:

    (Provide a list of all the services/products provided by the Company.)

12. **Assignment**

    The Company reserves the right to assign all or any part of its interest in and to this Agreement. The Consultant may not assign or transfer this Agreement, any interest therein or claim thereunder without the written approval of the Company.

13. **Integration**

    This Agreement, executed in duplicate, constitutes the entire contract between the parties and may be cancelled, modified or amended only by a written supplementary document executed by each of the parties hereto.

    IN WITNESS WHEREOF, the parties hereto have accepted and executed this Agreement this _____ day of _____ 20 _____

    ._____   _____

    John Smith, Consultant   ABC & Company
                    by: _____
                              (Authorized signatory)

Formal contract

A formal contract is preferred if the financial cost of the project is high, the project is complex, substantial financial commitment to suppliers or sub-consultants is involved, or it is the style of the client to require such a detailed contract.

Normally when government contracts are involved, the government prepares the formal contract.

Other situations where you might consider using a formal contract are when you have a new client, a client who has never used consulting services before, or a client who has a reputation for being difficult in general or complaining about fees in particular. Naturally, in this last case, if you have advance notice it would be very wise to reconsider any involvement with that client.

Sample 21 illustrates a formal contract. Table 3 is a checklist of provisions frequently covered in contracts with government or industry.

Sub-consulting agreement

This is an agreement between you and any sub-consultants you employ to undertake a part or all of a consulting project you have arranged.

It is quite common for consultants to subcontract work out to other consultants. You may use sub-consultants to keep overhead low, or if you are unable to perform the task yourself because you lack expertise in the area, or because a large project requires a large number of support resource personnel.

Generally you need not explain to your client that you are using sub-contracting services unless your client specifically asks. Sometimes a client would like to have the qualifications of a subcontractor clarified. All services performed by any sub-consultants are performed under your consulting company's name, and you are ultimately responsible for the quality of their work, so you must be very selective of who you hire and should monitor and approve all work they perform. In all outward respects, the sub-consultants are your employees under your direction. For example, all correspondence pertaining to the project should be printed only on your stationery.

Your subcontracting agreement should clearly spell out that the relationship of the sub-consultant to you is one of an independent contractor. You should also seriously consider a noncompetition clause in the contract that restricts the subcontractor's taking advantage of access to your clients to sell consulting services directly. A noncompetition clause or restrictive covenant can vary depending on the circumstances and the laws of your jurisdiction. Legal advice should be obtained before you complete

TABLE 3

DETAILED CONTRACT CHECKLIST
(COMMONLY USED FOR GOVERNMENT CONTRACTS)

General

1. Date of agreement.

2. Identification of client and consultant, including transfer of responsibility to successors (if the client is a public body, the authority under which it acts and the source of available funds should be specified).

3. Review of the background and brief definition of the project.

4. Scope of the assignment, including references to any detailed description incorporated in the appendices.

5. Effective date of commencement of work, when different from 1., and estimated or stipulated time for completion.

6. Designation of individuals in client and consultant organizations responsible for policy decisions.

7. Work statement containing a description of the requirements in detail. (The description should include the problem to be solved or the objective of the investigation, the approach or method to be used, and the extent or degree of work to be undertaken. The proposed statement of work should be sufficiently descriptive so as to become a usable yardstick.)

8. Provision for changes in the work requirements.

9. Provision for arbitration of disputes.

10. Provision for termination by either party for "cause" or "convenience".

Responsibilities of the consultant

1. Specify a project leader, professional help, services and information to be supplied.

2. Work schedule to be maintained.

3. Personnel to be supplied (may be detailed in appendix).

4. Availability for conferences with the client.

5. Reporting, including the schedule and nature of reports.

6. Ownership of designs, blueprints, reports etc, to be specified in the contract.

7. Safeguarding of information supplied by client.

8. Guarantee of performance, where required.

TABLE 3 *(Continued)*

9. Limitation of liability of the consultant with regard to the loss or damage of reports, third-party use of reports, errors or omissions or professional negligence (this provision for the benefit of the consultant).

10. Right to cancel the contract upon written notice of (x) days, provided that non-performance of the other party can be clearly documented and provided that the defaulting party has been given (x) days to make good non-performance.

11. Provision for disposal of any or all materials used in the performance of work.

Responsibilities of the client

1. Information, services and facilities to be provided.

2. Availability for conference with the consultant.

3. Number of days of staff support by client agency staff.

4. Prompt review and approval of reports and products.

5. Changes clause.

Duration of the contract

1. Stipulation of termination, either by stating a specific date, or by indicating the duration of the operation from the execution of the contract.

2. Provision and mechanism for the modification of the specified date by mutual agreement.

3. Provision for extension or renewal.

4. Provision and mechanism for early termination by either party.

5. Termination by reason of events beyond control of either party.

6. Provision against delays.

Financial provisions

1. Total financial commitment by the client.

2. Method and schedule of invoicing by the consultant.

3. Method of payment.

4. Currency or currencies of payment and conversion rates.

5. Guarantee of payment by the client.

6. Payment of interest on delayed payments.

TABLE 3 (Continued)

7. What are patent requirements? Who has the copyright in reports and other products? Who has publication rights and under what circumstances?

8. Payments shall be made within (x) days of invoicing, invoicing to be by arrangement.

9. Allowable costs or expenses to be invoiced separately from labour costs shall include but not be limited to:

   Telephone

   Postage and courier

   Travel

   Accommodation and miscellaneous

   Photocopying and printing

   Graphics

   Special typing support

   Translation

   Miscellaneous special materials

   Computer costs

   Subcontractual services

   Word processing

   Fax costs.

any contract so you can be certain that the noncompetition clause would be reasonably upheld as fair and appropriate if it were contested. The clause normally states that the sub-consultant shall not perform professional services independent of your firm to any of your clients past or present. The exception would be if the sub-consultant performs such services under your direct employ as an independent contractor. A two-year time period for the restriction is fairly common. The restriction covers a wide or narrow geographic base depending on the nature of your services.

A summary of the standard clauses that should be considered include:

(a) The parties to the contract

(b) Independent contractor status of sub-consultant

(c) The responsibilities of the sub-consultant fully specified

(d) Term of the contract

(e) Amount and method of payment for fees and expenses

(f) A cancellation provision in case the contract is cancelled

(g) The method and amount of remuneration to be paid to the sub-consultant up to the point of cancellation

(h) A confidentiality provision stating that all the client information accessible to the sub-consultant is to be held in strict confidence

(i) All documents obtained by the sub-consultant are to be returned to the consultant or client

(j) Provision that the contract cannot be assigned or duties delegated without the written consent of both parties

(k) Other 'standard' or 'unique' provisions.

The format of Sample 21, which shows a consultant contract, can also be used for a sub-consulting contract.

Agency agreement

An agency agreement is a contract that would be prepared if you were acting for a client as an external agent: for example, if you were selling a service on behalf of a client, or negotiating on behalf of the client with the government for funding purposes. The clauses in this type of contract vary considerably. Generally the client prepares the agreement for you to sign.

Letter of retainer agreement

This is an agreement that you outline in a letter. One form of retainer relationship is when you are available 'on call' at the request of a client based on need of your services. The consultant charges the client for being 'on call' and available, even though the consultant may not be used.

Another form of retainer relationship is if you provide a service on a periodic basis, for example monthly or quarterly.

PREPARING YOUR OWN CONTRACT

You should consider having several standardized contracts with variations depending on the different types of consulting services you perform. Space can be left in the contract for inserting the unique features of a specific consulting project. If your contracts are stored on a computer with word processing capabilities, each contract can easily be personalized in an original format for each consulting job.

The process of preparing your own contract is not difficult. Try to obtain as many sample forms of contracts as possible from your competitors and from contract books that are available from your local library or law school. Then refer to the various headings listed in this chapter or shown in the sample contracts or checklists. Outline the areas that you feel are important for your particular type of consulting services or problems. As soon as you have completed this exercise, expand on the points in a descriptive paragraph and then sub-divide into clauses in a format appropriate to your needs and in a style you prefer.

Take your draft contracts to your solicitor to evaluate. It is to your benefit to save your solicitor's time and your money by preparing the documents yourself. You are most familiar with your work and the important factors of your projects. Your solicitor can review your draft contracts and rewrite them or add additional clauses if required.

Major companies or government frequently have their own standardized contracts and send them to you for signature. In some cases there is room for negotiation; in other cases no negotiation is possible. If you are presented with the contract, you should review it thoroughly yourself and mark the areas that cause you concern. Also, note the areas that are not in the contract that you would prefer to have covered. Then discuss the contract with your solicitor. If you have any doubts about the required provisions of the contract, it is best to either negotiate to remove those provisions if possible, or turn down the project. If a contract is not completely to your liking, the degree of risk or dissatisfaction on your part or your client's part is high.

If a client wants to make changes to your contract, it is better to make them yourself rather than have a client make up his or her own contract. A client-prepared contract could have clauses or conditions you do not want.

In summary, attempt to prepare all your own contracts. This will establish the client–consultant relationship on your terms. Your initiative and leadership in preparing the contract should have a positive effect on the dynamics of the relationship with your client.

19

Time management

Like any other valuable resource, time can be managed. The better it is managed, the more productive and profitable your consulting business will be. All the other acquired skills you possess will lose much of their effectiveness if you are disorganized. As you probably will not have the time to attend to all the matters requiring your attention, you must ensure that the important tasks get done. Prioritize activities that generate continued profitability and future growth. By using some of the following proven techniques, your efficiency, productivity, and satisfaction will be increased considerably.

KEY STRATEGIES

Set priorities

Based on the goals you have established for your business, set your high, medium, and low priorities. Write them down. High-priority items are those that are vital to the business, have a deadline affixed to them, and usually need your personal attention. Medium-priority tasks are necessary to the business, but may not require your immediate attention; perhaps some of these tasks can be delegated. Low-priority items may be postponed to a more convenient time, or not done at all.

Keeping a 'to do' list provides a source of satisfaction and feeling of progress as items are crossed off. It can also alleviate the stress that results from trying to remember everything that has to be done.

Dealing with the high-priority items first is a particularly effective time management technique. By handling a critical task early in your day, you have the reward of feeling a sense of accomplishment. Often this provides additional motivation and drive to maintain the productivity momentum.

If there are unexpected interruptions, or minor problems arise, you are able to devote attention to them knowing that you have already dealt with your top-priority item. If on the other hand you defer your high-priority item until the afternoon, chances are that problems will arise that prevent you from getting to that high-priority task. As there can be a daily stream of unexpected interruptions, some people operate day after day in this time trap, never getting to those critical tasks.

In order to accomplish your high-priority tasks, it will be necessary to have a block of uninterrupted time. Hold all calls for the first hour of each day. Schedule other blocks of time necessary to fully complete a priority task.

Avoid procrastination. If one of your critical tasks doesn't have a built-in deadline, set one. In this way you will ensure that it gets to the top of your priority list. Perhaps you are having trouble starting a major project because it appears to be massive and you don't know where to begin. It is helpful to divide the major project into manageable stages. For instance, when preparing a bank loan proposal, one day's task may be to make a list of all the items you will include in your proposal. The other stages will be preparing each of the items on your list: sales projection charts, net worth statement, marketing concept, and so forth. Handling a large project in this manner of bite-size pieces, it is conceivable that the task could be accomplished within a week.

Be organized

If you make a habit of writing everything in your desk or diary and daily diary as soon as you become aware of an event, you will avoid double-booking appointments or forgetting them. You may decide to schedule your appointments for the afternoon whenever possible, to allow your morning to be a free block of time during which you can accomplish items on your 'to do' list. When scheduling your workday, allow yourself some flexibility and leeway, as things don't always go according to plan. Allow sufficient time so that each task can be carried out in a thorough, unhurried manner.

Having an up-to-date and efficient filing system will enable you to find your files quickly. On the other hand, keeping every piece of paper that comes across your desk in an escalating stack, or in overstuffed files, only creates frustration and delay when you are trying to locate a piece of information. Of course you will need to keep a copy of your important correspondence, proposals, and bookkeeping records. But filing space is expensive. Before filing a piece of paper you need to ask yourself: Will I ever have to refer back to this? Can I get another copy of this if sometime in the future I need to refer to it?

There is much to be said for the person who is able to keep a tidy workspace. While many defend their cluttered desks by saying, 'I know exactly where everything is', it is well known how much time is wasted shuffling papers. The hidden time waster is the distraction created by a cluttered work area. Instead of having a clear train of thought when working on the critical priority items, a casual glance at the clutter may trigger numerous reminders of things that must be done. This could create unnecessary delays in completing the immediate task, as well as cause extra stress and a feeling of being overwhelmed.

Being prepared for meetings and appointments saves time otherwise spent in prolonged discussions. Before the meeting you should review your file, make notes, prepare an agenda, and stick to it. Anticipating potential problems will enable you to have an action plan ready to implement, rather than merely reacting to events as they occur.

Delegate

As your company expands, you may need to increase staff, contract out for employees, or have consulting associates. It will be necessary for you to delegate to others some of your responsibilities. At times, it will appear easier to do it yourself than to train, supervise, and check someone else's work. Delegating the authority builds staff morale, competence and motivation.

Learn to say no. You may receive a request, for example to participate in a community activity, that will require taking time from your business day. Knowing your daily workload and having the ability to say no is important to your time management.

Be decisive

Preciseness in identifying problems and decisiveness in the actions to be taken will save time in your workday. Similar to the technique used with large or insurmountable tasks, by breaking a problem down into different parts you can see more clearly the root of the problem. To resolve it, list the various alternatives and rate the degree of effectiveness of each. Practising this technique will help you develop the ability to go through this process quickly in your mind. This will enhance your effectiveness in resolving small problems before they escalate into larger ones.

The art of speaking and writing concisely is a time saver for you and your associates. It will also foster improved communication between you and your staff, and customers. The effective use of e-mail and voice mail messaging can greatly enhance your time management.

AVOIDING TIME WASTERS

Using voice mail effectively

Voice mail allows customers to send messages to you directly. It creates a better impression than a telephone answering machine, and is far more versatile. A full 75 per cent of all business calls are not completed on the first attempt. The effect is an incredible amount of wasted time and energy. Here are some prime examples of the benefits of voice mail:

▌   *Communicates more efficiently*. Lets people communicate the complete message without regard for confidentiality or complexity of the information. Messages are in the caller's own voice, with all the original intonations and inflections.

▌   *Saves time and money on long distance charges*. When messages are left on voice mail, calls are invariably shorter, as the caller gets right to the point. Live communications encourage less chit chat, thereby wasting time and money. When you are out of town, you can call into the voice mail to receive your messages at times when the long distance rates are lower.

▌   *Increases productivity of staff*. Instead of staff answering many phone calls or taking messages, staff can be more efficient and do additional tasks or provide more personal service to callers who wish to bypass the voice mail and speak directly to a receptionist or secretary.

▌   *Cuts down on paging and holding times*. The caller can go directly to a voice mailbox rather than waiting on hold.

▌   *Voice mail/auto attendant works 365 days a year, 24 hours a day*. You can phone in any time from anywhere to receive your messages, with a confidential access number. The voice mail system can route callers to appropriate voice mail boxes, take messages, play customized greetings depending on the time of day or evening, offer other mail box menu selections for specific information, and perform many other features, as noted below.

▌   *Automatic paging of all voice mail messages*. Your voice mail can be programmed to call you as soon as messages are left on the service. You can leave instructions as to where calls should be directed (mobile, pager, home, or associate's number) as they are received.

▌   *Fax response option*. This means that a caller can phone a voice mail box number, input his or her fax number, and instantly your fax message is transmitted to the caller's fax machine. You can store any number of pages on the computer to be transmitted automatically upon request.

Using e-mail effectively

Similar to voice mail, but in the written form, e-mail can be a great time saver when used effectively:

▪ Communicating with others in different time zones is greatly enhanced with e-mail. The business day virtually becomes 24 hours.

▪ Costs are considerably less as there are no long distance telephone charges. Messages are briefer and to the point. The formalities typical of business letter writing are omitted and replaced by informal greetings and sign-offs.

▪ Formatting is simplified and expedient, with less time being spent making it look nice for the reader, as with business letters.

▪ When receiving an e-mail message, it is quick and easy to send a brief acknowledgement or reply by selecting the 'reply to' option on the e-mail program menu. The recipient's address as well as your own is automatically inserted for you.

▪ It is easy to send a copy of the message to other parties for their information, action or response by adding their e-mail addresses. In this way, you can receive group feedback on a proposal within a short time frame.

Too many telephone calls

Ensure that written and verbal telephone messages are complete. Knowing not only the name and phone number of the person calling but also the purpose of the call enables you to deal with the response quickly and effectively, often delegating the response to someone else. Bunch your calls before lunch or towards the end of the day when people are less likely to chat. Use fax, e-mail, or voice mail messages instead of a telephone call where one-way transfer of information is all that is required.

Overscheduling/too many things to do

Concentrate on important items and disregard the trivial. Use your diary to plan your day and prepare a priority list of tasks. Learn to say no. Delegate.

Too much paper

Deal with each piece of paper only once. If it is junk mail, throw it out. Request to be taken off the distribution list of unknown faxes and junk e-mail. If it is for the file, file it immediately. If it requires a response, a handwritten response or a telephone call may suffice. Or delegate routine matters to another staff member. By handling your morning mail in this manner, you will avoid tomorrow's task of dealing with the paperwork you set aside today.

Scheduled meetings

Be certain they start and end on time, and follow the agenda. Keep on topic. Ensure that a summary is given, noting any action to be taken after the meeting and by whom.

Perfectionism

Striving for excellence is healthy, gratifying, and attainable. However, aiming for perfection is frustrating, neurotic, and a waste of time.

20

Expanding your practice

There are many ways to acquire clients. The simplest way is to keep your existing clients happy and nurture the present and past clients well. Studies show that over 70 per cent of a consultant's business is based on repeat business or referral business from existing clients. A marketing formula shows that the average person has over 200 contacts including friends, relatives, and associates. By carefully developing this client potential you can expand your practice rapidly.

For example, from one satisfied client you could obtain numerous projects – sufficient to keep you busy on an ongoing basis. If your client gives you repeat work on a regular basis and also recommends you to ten other business associates in the same industry, and if five of those ten become clients, your business will grow. Former employees of the first client or referral clients may go to work for other firms in the private or public sector. If they enjoyed working with you, they will request your services again or refer work to you. The possibilities are limitless.

An effective way of keeping your clients satisfied is to create client dependency. The more the client relies on you because of your specialization, the more repeat business you will generate. The more your client respects you for your knowledge and leadership, the more the client will look to you for guidance.

It is important that the client feels in control at all times. You must maintain your image as a unique commodity. Your role is to complement staff. You do not want to be perceived as just another member of staff.

If there are particular tasks that the client does not enjoy, and if you have the skills and ability to perform those tasks and fill the void (and if the situation seems appropriate), you can create further dependency. If the outcome of a project is particularly successful and considerable positive feedback occurs, make a point of having your client share the glory with you. A satisfied client will appreciate your value and provide you with more consulting contracts.

There are other ways of developing your practice. Expanding your line by adding additional services that are natural extensions of your first service is an effective method. If you have clients that retain you for one service, you are creating a potential two- or three-fold growth pattern with all your clientele. Because you already have credibility with the clients for one project, it will be much easier for you to market your skills for the other services.

Subcontracting is another way of expanding your practice. You can locate subcontractors from your network and through referral. They can be effectively used to increase your earnings by providing depth and greater capacity for your business. You would be in a position to make proposals for larger or more complex projects using past, present, or future clients as your base. If a client has been satisfied with your service on a smaller project or a particular service line, and you have additional service lines and a greater depth and capacity, the prospects are endless. Naturally, subcontracting will involve more administration for you, but the independent contractor status of sub-consultants will allow you flexibility to hire them on an as-needed basis.

Other ways to expand your practice are to review all aspects of your operation on an ongoing basis, note the weak areas, and develop a specific plan for dealing with them. Improvement in areas such as self-promotion and more efficient follow up on leads can also enhance your clientele base.

Appendix 1

Sources of reference information for consultants

Analytical Unit, Small Business Service, Level 1 St Mary's House, c/o Moorfoot, Sheffield S1 4PQ (fax: 0114 279 4477; e-mail: statistics@ sbs.gsi.gov.uk).

Barclays Bank (barclays.com) – website pages on services for small, medium and large businesses.

British Consultants and Construction Bureau (www.bccb.org.uk) – 'an independent, non-profit Association based in London, with strong political and commercial links around the world. It regularly liaises with foreign governments and the private sector to identify commercial opportunities for its members'.

British Venture Capital Association (www.bvca.co.uk) – 'represents around 165 UK-based private equity and venture capital firms, the vast majority of all such firms in the UK. The BVCA is the public face of the industry providing services to its members, investors and entrepreneurs as well as the Government and media'.

Business Link (www.businesslink.gov.uk) – practical advice for business: an essential resource of information and reference on all issues related to starting up and running a business. Hotline – tel: 0845 600 9006.

Chartered Institute of Marketing (www.cim.co.uk) – resources include small business solutions, 'helping you to grow your business by selling more to more people, both on the internet and through conventional channels to market'.

Chartered Institute of Public Finance and Accountancy (www.cipfa.org.uk) – source of detailed information on the commissioning of consultancy and other services by local authorities in the UK.

Ethnic Minority Business Forum (www.ethnicbusiness.org) – the role of this forum is to help ensure that ethnic minority businesses are given the right help and advice to succeed.

Federation of Small Businesses (www.fsb.org.uk) – 'the voice of the small business sector'.

Forum of Private Business (www.fpb.co.uk) – 'a not-for-profit pressure group, driven by its membership and representing over 25,000 businesses in the UK who between them employ 600,000 people. Offers a wide range of business solutions and benefits to help its membership grow successfully and profitably'.

HM Customs and Excise (www.hmce.gov.uk) – information on VAT, importing and exporting issues.

HSBC (www.hsbc.com) – business banking pages on website.

Inland Revenue (www.inlandrevenue.gov.uk) – comprehensive and authoritative information on taxation issues.

Institute for Small Business Affairs (www.isba.co.uk) – set up to encourage the conduct of high quality research in the field of small business development and to assist and inform those responsible for the formulation, development, implementation and evaluation of enterprise policy.

Institute of Directors (www.iod.com) – 'as a worldwide association of members, the Institute of Directors provides a network that reaches into every corner of the business community'.

Labour Market Statistics (www.statistics.gov.uk) Helpline, Office for National Statistics (tel: 020 7533 6176; e-mail: labour.market@ons.gov.uk).

Lloyds TSB (www.lloydstsb.com) – business banking pages on website.

Local Business Partnerships – 'Local Business Partnerships provide a framework to enable the business community and local authorities to work together to streamline the regulation process. The aim is to make it easier for the businessperson to understand and comply with regulations'. Contact through local Chamber of Commerce or local authority.

Management Consultancies Association (www.mca.org.uk) – 'the trade association for leading management consulting firms in the UK'.

National Business Angels Network Information Hotline – tel: 020 7329 4141: informal investors in business.

National Federation of Enterprise Agencies (www.nfea.com) – 'the membership body for local enterprise agencies in England. It forms a network of independent, not for profit local agencies committed to responding to the needs of small and growing businesses by providing a comprehensive range of quality services'.

NatWest (www.natwest.com) – website pages for business banking and downloadable business guides.

Office for National Statistics – comprehensive source of government statistics.

Office of Government Commerce (www.ogc.gov.uk) – 'works with government to improve procurement and project/programme management and with suppliers to make the government marketplace more efficient and attractive to business'.

Official Journal of the European Communities (Supplement S) – information on tenders for public sector contracts, updated daily and available online at http://ted.publications.eu.int

Professional Contractors' Group (www.pcgroup.org.uk) – 'the representative body for the freelance small business community ... dedicated to protecting and promoting the interests of this community.' Publications include a free Guide to Freelancing.

Sector Skills Development Agency (www.ssda.org.uk) – 'established to underpin the UK-wide network of Sector Skills Councils which bring together employers, trade unions and professional bodies working with government to develop the skills that UK business needs'.

UK Business Incubation (www.ukbi.co.uk) – 'champions the interests of the business incubation industry, by spreading good practice and setting standards of incubation. By being a catalyst for innovation, development and change we will increase the survival and growth of new business ideas'.

Appendix 2

Proposal evaluation checklist

GENERAL FACTORS

(a) Has the bidder responded with an appropriate technique or is he or she trying to fit the problem to a favourite technique?

(b) What priority will this project receive from the consultant? How important will it be to his or her firm?

(c) Does the proposal meet the terms of reference and the intended scope of the study?

(d) How useful or capable of implementation will the end product be?

(e) What degree of originality is present in the proposal?

(f) Are the submission of progress reports and presentation of interim briefings required? What progress reports and interim briefings are planned?

(g) What degree of direct consultant–client liaison is proposed? Does the consultant–client relationship include a training component for the client's personnel? What type of training is proposed?

(h) Is the proposed content of progress reports in accordance with the requirements of the client? Will progress reports contain a monthly statement of costs incurred, commitments, and, if necessary, a revised estimate of total costs?

(i) When the project is complete, how does the consultant intend to hand over the project?

(j) What degree of follow up and/or debriefing is proposed? To whom do the relevant data belong and what happens to them when the project is completed?

PERFORMANCE

(a) Is the usual business of the consultant closely related to the proposed work?

(b) Do the references to past experience include activities specifically related to the requirements of the proposed study?

(c) Has the bidder been honoured by professional societies because of the performance in a specific professional area?

(d) What reputation does the firm hold in the area of the proposed study?

(e) Has the firm worked for this client before, and if so with what success?

(f) Are the statements of past performance worded in a meaningful way so you can identify what work was actually performed?

(g) Are there aspects of past performance that indicate particular weaknesses or strengths?

SCOPE OF WORK

(a) Has the proposal demonstrated an understanding of the problems to be solved?

(b) Is this research area new to the company?

(c) Has the bidder made an accurate assessment of the problem based on an interpretation of the requirements put forth in the work statement?

(d) Has the bidder presented an approach that will achieve the stated objectives?

(e) Is the proposed approach supported with justification of why it should achieve the evaluation objectives?

(f) Do you think the suggested approach will work?

(g) Has the bidder introduced unanticipated events which may result in a project overrun or an expanded scope of work?

(h) Does the proposal differentiate between the simpler and the more difficult performance requirements?

(i) Does the proposal convincingly show a depth of understanding of the problem?

(j) Are the technical problems clearly delineated or are they merely 'parroted' from the proposal request?

(k) Have the limits of the problems been specified to show that the proposed study will be restricted to an appropriate scope?

(l) Is there a concise but adequate review of literature? Is the literature review an annotated bibliography or is it a scholarly critique?

(m) Are the specific objectives of the proposal clearly stated? Are these goals realistic in view of time, equipment, budget, and professional experience of the principal investigator?

(n) Does the plan, in fact, permit an unequivocal test of the stated hypotheses of research questions?

(o) Does the proposal represent a unique, imaginative approach?

(p) Is the technical programme fully responsive to all written requirements and specifications?

(q) Are there any apparent discrepancies or omissions?

(r) Are the 'products' clearly defined and presented?

PERSONNEL

(a) Is it clear which tasks in the study will be assigned to specific personnel and for what amount of time?

(b) Are the personnel assigned to specific tasks qualified by training and experience to successfully perform the tasks?

(c) Is there a clear organization chart depicting project management? Is the apportionment of personnel level and time to specific tasks realistic?

(d) What assurances are made concerning the availability of personnel proposed? Was a contingency plan requested if certain personnel become unavailable?

(e) Have enough time and personnel been included to provide adequate administrative management of the study?

(f) Is the author of the proposal one of the key personnel?

(g) Does the success of the project depend, to a large degree, upon personnel not directly associated with the prospective firm?

(h) Do biographies relate specific experience of personnel to the specific needs of this project?

(i) Does the proposal show the capabilities of the management to handle a project of the size contemplated?

(j) Are the position of the programme manager in the overall organization and the limits of his or her authority and responsibility shown?

(k) Are the type, frequency, and effectiveness of management controls and method for corrective action shown?

(l) Does the task organization integrate the overall organization in terms of effective integration of research, development, design, drafting, technical writing, and, where appropriate, test functions?

(m) Is it clearly demonstrated that top-level management will continue a high level of interest and assume responsibility for successful accomplishment of the programme?

(n) Is the proposal dependent on recruitment of key personnel?

PLANNING AND MANAGEMENT

(a) Has the work schedule been specified clearly, and is it realistic in terms of time and money? Does it fit with available personnel?

(b) If the time of performance is important and is a competitive evaluation factor, is the proposed schedule supported by the technical proposal?

(c) Is the planning realistic? Does it follow recognized and accepted procedure?

(d) Does the proposal show that the delivery schedule will be met and how it will be met?

(e) Is sufficient detail regarding master scheduling, programming, follow up, and other such functions given to reinforce the foregoing assurance?

(f) Are the various technical phases of the project detailed and realistically scheduled?

(g) Are effective review, evaluation, and control provided at specific checkpoints?

FACILITIES

(a) Are the facilities and equipment needed for successful completion of the study specified in the proposal?

(b) How does the bidder intend to access facilities not at the contractor's site?

(c) Does the use of facilities outside of the contractor's firm require a subcontract? If so, is the proposed subcontractor specifically mentioned, along with an explanation of its required qualifications?

(d) Is the planned use of facilities, such as printing, data processing, etc., realistic?

(e) If computer services are required, are there controls built into the processing so corrective action can be taken at intermittent points if necessary?

(f) Is any government-furnished equipment needed?

(g) Are the proposed laboratory and test facilities adequate for the requirements of the technical scope?

(h) Are resources overly committed?

COST

(a) Is the overall cost within range of your (the contracting agency's) budget?

(b) What is the relationship between the cost figures and equivalent items in the technical proposal?

(c) Are the personnel costs reasonable according to the tasks to be performed?

(d) Are the appropriate personnel assigned to perform the appropriate tasks?

(e) Have expenditures been set aside for subcontracting requirements such as data processing?

(f) If a large-scale questionnaire must be mailed, has an adequate sum been set aside for postage?

(g) Have costs for development of instruments and purchase of materials such as scoring sheets, etc., been included?

(h) Does the travel seem reasonable when compared to the tasks to be accomplished?

(i) If consultants or experts are included, is their daily rate reasonable and within the proper financial range? Is the proposed time reasonable?

(j) Is an appropriate type of contract requested?

(k) Is the schedule of payment acceptable?

(l) Have appropriate procedures been used to estimate costs?

Appendix 3

Further reading from Kogan Page

Bids, Tenders and Proposals: Winning business through best practice, 2002, Harold Lewis

Consultant - Market Yourself: Raise your profile and attract new business, 2002, Robert Gentle

Consultants & Advisers: A best practice guide to choosing, using & getting good value, 2004, Harold Lewis

The Effective Director: The essential guide to director and board development, 2001, Chris Pierce

How to be Your Own Management Consultant: Consultancy tools and techniques to improve your business, 2001, Calvert Markham

How to Succeed as an Independent Consultant: Work with your clients and promote your business, 2002, Timothy R V Foster

Management Consultancy: A handbook for best practice, 2nd edn, 2001, Philip Sadler

Management Consulting in Practice: Award-winning international case studies, 2004, Fiona Czerniawska and Paul May

The Top Consultant, 4th edn, 2004, Calvert Markham

ALSO PUBLISHED BY KOGAN PAGE

A Handbook of Management Techniques: The best selling guide to modern management methods, 3rd edn, 2001, Michael Armstrong

Advanced Project Management, 2004, Alan Orr

Bridging the Culture Gap: A practical guide to international business communication, 2004, Penny Carté and Chris Fox

Building Tomorrow's Company: A guide to sustainable business success, 2002, Philip Sadler

The Business Enterprise Handbook, revised edn, 2003, Robert Brown and Liz Clarke

The Business Plan Workbook, 2001, Robert Brown, Colin Barrow and Paul Barrow

Business Solutions on Demand: Creating customer value at the speed of light, 2004, Mark Cerasale and Merlin Stone

Change for the Best, 2004, Sarah Cook

Change Management Excellence: The 5 essentials of successful organizational change, 2004, Sarah Cook Steve Macaulay and Hilary Coldicott

Creative Business Presentations: Inventive ideas for making an instant impact, 2003, Eleri Sampson

Cross-cultural Communication: The essential guide to international management, 2003, John Mattock

Customer Care Excellence: How to create an effective customer focus, 4th edn, 2002, Sarah Cook

The Customer Service Workbook, 2002, Neviulle Lake and Kristin Hickey

Financial Management for the Small Business, 2001, Colin Barrow

Forming a Limited Company: A Practical Guide to Legal Requirements and Procedures, 8th edn, 2004, Patricia Clayton

Goal Directed Project Management, 3rd edn, 2004, Coopers & Lybrand

Going Public: The essential guide to flotation, 2002, Jonathan Reuvid

Growing a Private Company: Commercial strategies for building a business worth millions, 2000, Ian Smith

The Handbook of Project Management: A practical guide to effective policies and procedures, 2nd edn, 2003, Trevor L Young

Hard-core Management: What you wont learn from the business gurus, 2003, Jo Owen

Having Their Cake: How the city and big bosses are consuming UK business, 2004, Pat Scott and Don Young

The Healthy Organization: A revolutionary approach to people and management, 2nd edn, 2004, Brian Dive

How to Be an Even Better Manager: A complete A to Z of proven techniques & essential skills, 6th edn, 2004, Michael Armstrong

How to Prepare a Business Plan: Planning for Successful Start-up and Expansion, 4th edn2004, Edward Blackwell

The Inspirational Leader: How to motivate, encourage and achieve success, 2003, John Adair

Law for the Small Business, 2004, Patricia Clayton

Management Stripped Bare: What they don't teach you at business school, 2002, Jo Owen

Managing People in a Small Business, 2002, John Stredwick

Not Bosses But Leaders: How to lead the way to success, 3rd edn, 2002, John Adair

The Practice of Project Management: A guide to the business-focussed approach, 2002, Dennis Comninos and Enzo Frigenti

Project Risk Management: An essential tool for managing & controlling projects, 2004, D van Well-Stam, F Lindenaar, S van Kinderen and BP van den Bunt

Starting a Successful Business, 4th edn, 2001, Michael Morris

Strategic Business Planning: A dynamic system for improving performance and competitive advantage, 2nd edn, 2004, Clive Reading

Strategic Planning Workbook, 2002, Neville Lake

Successful Marketing for the Small Business, 5th edn, 2001, Dave Patten

Ultimate Business Presentations Book, 2003, Martin Yate and Peter Sander

The above titles are available from all good bookshops or direct from the publishers. To obtain more information, please contact the publisher at the address below:

Kogan Page
120 Pentonville Road
London N1 9JN
Tel: 020 7278 0433
Fax: 020 7837 6348
www.kogan-page.co.uk

Index